KIDS EXPLORE AMERICA'S CATHOLIC HERITAGE

Young Writers Workshop

Pauline

BOOKS & MEDIA

Boston

Nihil Obstat: Rev. William T. Kelley, S.T.D.
Imprimatur: ✠ Bernard Cardinal Law
Archbishop of Boston
October 5, 2001

Library of Congress Cataloging-in-Publication Data

Kids explore America's Catholic heritage / Young Writers Workshop.
        p. cm.
Summary: A simple presentation of America's Catholic heritage and culture written
and illustrated by students from grades four to seven. Includes chapters on various
aspects of Catholic faith and worship, personal stories, recipes, and crafts.
    ISBN 0-8198-4208-7 (pbk.)
  1. Catholic Church—United States—History—Juvenile literature. 2. United
States—Church history—Juvenile literature. 3. Catholic Church—Doctrines—
Juvenile literature. [1. Catholic Church. 2. Children's writings. 3. Children's art.]
I. Young Writers Workshop.
    BX1406.3 .K53 2002
    282'.73—dc21
                                        2001006415

The authors and publisher wish to thank the Sisters of the Blessed Sacrament, Catholic
News Service, James Baca, Ron Horn, Lillian LaFleur and Al Mida for their gracious permission
to use the photographs which appear in this book.

Cover design: Regina Frances Dick, FSP

Printed and published in the U.S.A. by Pauline Books & Media, 50 Saint Pauls Avenue,
Boston, MA 02130-3491.

www.pauline.org

Pauline Books & Media is the publishing house of the Daughters of St. Paul, an international congregation of women religious serving the Church with the communications
media.

1 2 3 4 5 6 7   07 06 05 04 03 02

CONTENTS

TEACHERS' PREFACE

Kids Explore America's Catholic Heritage is the eighth book in the *Kids Explore Series.* It was written in a summer workshop at Saint Louis School in Englewood, Colorado. The writing process required the 105 students, 39 teachers, 13 high school mentors, and numerous volunteers to focus their thoughts and energy on their Catholic faith. This focus brought out beautiful details of the faith which were not readily apparent beforehand. These revelations would have been exciting even in a vacuum, but in the workshop setting we were able to share them, thus multiplying the experience a hundredfold. The result was an exponential growth in our belief in the love of Jesus Christ for us and for the Catholic Church.

During these ten days we celebrated a Penance service, had Eucharistic adoration, prayed together at Mass, sang religious songs, participated in art and cooking projects, heard numerous speakers, did research, and, of course, wrote.

Our young authors, students in grades four through seven, enriched their knowledge of the Catholic faith and developed their writing talents in the process. The teachers in the program furthered their teaching skills through a graduate course offered by Benedictine College in Atchison, Kansas.

Before beginning to read this book, it is important to recognize some key Catholic beliefs. We believe that Jesus is the Son of God who came into the world to teach us, establish the Church and give his life for us. We believe that the Bible is the Word of God. We believe in the mystery of the Holy Trinity—one God in three divine Persons: Father, Son and Holy Spirit. We believe that the Eucharist is the real Body and Blood of Jesus Christ, not just a symbol. We also believe that God calls us to enjoy his happiness forever, even after death. Additionally, we believe that by belonging to the Catholic Church and receiving the sacraments, we receive special grace from God to help us reach heaven. As Catholics we share some of our beliefs with members of other religions. We share many of our beliefs with other Christians, like our Orthodox and Protestant brothers and sisters. We pray that one day soon all Christians may be united.

By reading this book you will gain insight into Catholicism from a child's point of view. Whether you want to find a hands-on craft, learn about miracles, review the meaning behind the seven sacraments, learn what it is like to grow up Catholic, explore the life of a saint, review the different parts of the Mass, discover ways to put your faith into action or take a look at American history from a Catholic perspective, it is all here for you to enjoy.

We hope you absorb the love expressed by the children. It permeates every page and radiates from every paragraph of this book. The simple language of the children leaves no doubt about their love for Jesus and the Catholic Church. They celebrate that love in their writing as they did in their lives during the workshop.

Jesus has told us that where two or three are gathered in his name, he is there also. In this workshop, we wish to thank the Lord for his presence, helping and guiding us in a special way. We wish to thank all of the people who helped make this book possible. You can find the names of the participants and volunteers in the back of the book. It is our hope that we will continue to celebrate the Lord's love every day, as we did during the workshop. Most of all, we hope that by reading our book, you will be inspired to join us in this celebration.

HISTORY

*Our country's Catholic history
Is too long to all fit here.
Don't let it stay a mystery…
Do more research during the year!*

There is so much Catholic history that we could not write about all of it. We decided to include a timeline in our chapter and just tell you about some of the main points. If you find an item on the timeline that you are interested in, you could research it more. Just remember, there is so much more history that we didn't even include on the timeline.

History is important because it helps to explain who we are and what we believe. History is very important to Christians because it includes the life of Jesus Christ. Jesus, God's own Son, lived and preached in Galilee. Jesus' relationship with God was simple, direct and available to all. His love of God was so fantastic that he spent his whole life telling it. Jesus called his Father "Abba" (this word means "My dear papa"). Jesus taught about the problems that people had like poverty, hunger, illness and injustice. He liked to be with all kinds of people.

We wouldn't know about our traditions if it weren't for history. Our calendar wouldn't even be the same if it were not for Jesus. We date all time in our world from the birth of Jesus Christ. "B.C."

Jennifer Bissel

YEAR EVENTS

1 MODERN DATES BEGIN WITH JESUS

33 JESUS BEGINS CATHOLIC CHURCH

means *Before Christ.* "A.D." means *Anno Domini*—"in the year of the Lord." A.D. dates are those that came after the birth of Jesus. (All the dates on our timeline are A.D. dates.) We know Jesus through history. If we did not know about our past, our future would not be important to us. We would not care if we had two billion bucks.

WHO ARE WE AND HOW DID WE BEGIN?

The Early Church

What does the word Catholic mean? The word Catholic means universal, worldwide. Catholic means everywhere, not one church, not one city, not one state. It means everywhere.

Was Jesus the first Catholic? YES! In the Bible, Jesus told his apostles: "Full authority has been given to me both in heaven and on earth; go therefore and make disciples of all the nations" (Mt 28:18-19). The Catholic Church began with Jesus!

How did the Pope come about? In the Bible, we know that Jesus said who the first Pope was. Here is the exact quote from the Bible that tells the story of Jesus

talking to his apostle Peter: "I for my part declare to you, you are the 'rock', and on this rock I will build my church, and the jaws of death shall not prevail against it" (Mt 16:18). There have been 262 Popes (bishops of Rome) since Peter.

Who said the first Mass? Jesus did! The first Mass was celebrated on the night before Jesus died, and that Mass is called the Last Supper. Saint Justin was the first person we know of to call the prayers and worship by the early Christians a "Mass." He gave us this word in the early part of the second century A.D. The letter he wrote so long ago describes the Mass

in detail and sounds just like our Mass today.

Where did we get the Catholic Bible? The early Christians used the same Scriptures as the Jews. But the people passed around the stories that Jesus told while he was on earth. They also told about the miracles that he did. Saint Paul wrote many letters to his friends in the cities that he visited. He told everybody about Jesus so that they would believe that Jesus is the Christ, the Son of God. There were so many letters and stories about Jesus that the Pope called all Catholic bishops to meet in Rome in 382

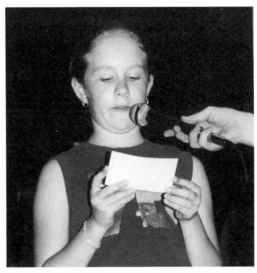

Young authors share what they learned about the history of the Catholic Church

A.D. This group selected the Christian letters and stories to be included in the Bible. This part of the Bible is now called the New Testament.

At first, it was very dangerous to be a Christian. For the first 300 years after Jesus, many Christians had to choose between life and death. Those who died for their faith are called martyrs. The martyrs have been special heroes to Catholics. They gave up their lives because they believed in Jesus! The year 64 A.D. was a very special year. The Christians began to be killed by the Romans. Saint Peter

and Saint Paul were killed at this time by the Roman Emperor Nero because they would not worship Nero as a god. Saint Ignatius of Antioch was a Christian leader at the end of the first century and beginning of the second. On his way to Rome to be killed for his faith, he wrote letters to his friends. He was the first person to use the word "Catholic" to describe people who believe in Jesus. Among the first martyrs there were many women. Two of these famous women who died for their faith are Saint Perpetua and her maid Saint Felicity. Both of them got

Writing takes concentration!

killed in the Roman amphitheater just because they believed in Jesus.

Saints are Catholics who are very good examples for other people to follow. Saint Helena was one of our earliest saints. She was the mother of the Roman Emperor Constantine. After she became Catholic, she influenced her son to make it legal to be a Catholic. She spent her money to help the poor and to build churches. When she was very old, she went to Jerusalem to find the Holy Cross—the one that Jesus died on. She found it and built a church on Mount Calvary. Another great early saint was Monica, the mother of Saint Augustine. She prayed and prayed for years that her son would give up his bad life and become a Catholic. He did!

For a long time it was against the law to be a Christian, but the early Church still grew swiftly. In the year 313 A.D., the Roman Emperor Constantine passed the Edict of Milan agreeing that Christianity could be practiced freely. He was one of the first emperors who accepted the Christian faith.

In 354 A.D., Saint Augustine worked really hard studying the philosophy and theology of the Catholic Church. He became a bishop and worked tirelessly for the Catholic Church by preaching, ministering, and writing.

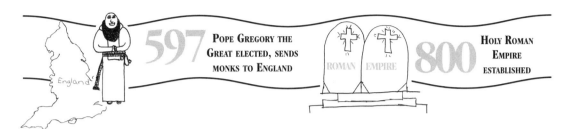

597 POPE GREGORY THE GREAT ELECTED, SENDS MONKS TO ENGLAND

800 HOLY ROMAN EMPIRE ESTABLISHED

The Church in the Early and Middle Ages

As soon as Pope Leo III crowned Charlemagne the new emperor of France on Christmas of 800 A.D., the relationship between the Church and the state became official. The Holy Roman Empire began. The Popes became great powers not only in the Church but also in the government during the earlier part of the Middle Ages. But in 1054 a sad event called the East-West Schism took place. This is when Catholics living in Constantinople decided not to obey the Pope anymore. The word "schism" means "tear." This event was a tear in the unity of the Church.

In Catholic churches long ago, people had to stand or sit on the floor because there were no pews. During the Middle Ages many new things were introduced. Churches were built in the shape of a cross. The three steps up to the altar were to remind the people of the Father, the Son, and the Holy Spirit. The most important part of the church was the choir. Rosaries as well as statues and paintings of the saints became popular. Plays and religious dramas were acted out in public. Monasteries and convents brought the Catholic faith to many places.

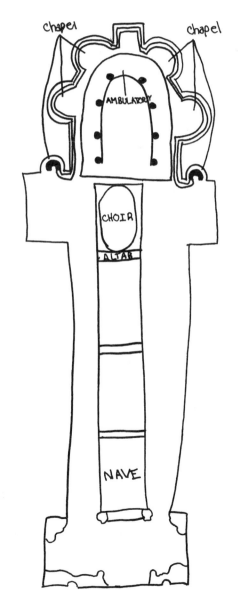

1054 — EAST-WEST SCHISM   1095 — CRUSADES BEGIN

The Crusades—a series of battles fought by European Christians to regain or defend Christian lands—happened at the beginning of the Middle Ages. In 1095, Pope Urban II proclaimed a crusade or holy war to free Palestine and the Holy Land from the Muslim Turks. He promised Catholics that they would inherit Paradise if they would take up the cross for God's cause. There were eight crusades over the next 200 years. One was even called the Children's Crusade! Those who fought in these wars were called Crusaders. As time went on, some of the Crusaders no longer acted for the right purpose. Instead, they went to battle because they wanted money and power. This led to problems.

Did the early Catholic Church have troubles? Sadly, yes. There was a struggle for leadership between the bishops of Rome and Constantinople. Eventually the Christian world was divided by the Schism of 1054 into the Roman Catholic Church in the West and the Orthodox Church in the East. For about the last 1,000 years, eastern Orthodox Christians have continued to have many of the same beliefs as Roman Catholics, but they do not acknowledge the Pope as the head of the Church.

In 1517, on October 31, a German monk by the name of Martin Luther made a list of ninety-five complaints against the

Church. He nailed them to a church door in the city of Wittenberg, Germany. This was the beginning of the Protestant Reformation, when the Christian Church in western Europe split into two groups, the Catholics and the Protestants.

The Pope knew there was a big problem, so he called the bishops to the Council of Trent to see what needed to be done. From 1545 to 1563 bishops met to say strongly that Jesus Christ wants both belief in Catholic teachings and good works. The bishops also passed reforms that would change the course of the Catholic Church for the next 400 years. Many changes were made. An important one was stopping the selling of indulgences. An example of an indulgence would be going to Mass every Friday for nine weeks and you would get a gift from God for your soul. The selling of indulgences was where a priest or monk would say, for example, "Instead of saying five prayers every day for a month, you will get grace if you give me $100." Some of the positive changes from the council included prayer books for the people to use at Mass, increased devotion to Mary and schools for the proper training of priests.

Columbus, Natives, Conquistadors, Guadalupe

Christopher Columbus thought the earth was round and he wanted to prove it. Columbus asked kings to give him money so he could find a shortcut to India, but they all said no. A friend told Columbus that he knew Queen Isabella of Spain. The friend talked to the queen and she decided to give Columbus ships and crews. In the year 1492, Christopher Columbus sailed from Spain to try to find India. The three ships Columbus sailed on were called the Santa Maria, the Pinta and the Nina. They did not reach India but they found an island that Columbus named Hispaniola. Spain's main religion was Catholicism. Christopher Columbus claimed his discoveries for Spain and his God.

Along with conquistadors (conquerors) from Spain, missionaries came whose

main interest was to convert Natives to Catholicism. The missionaries did this in many ways. Sometimes, the conquistadors would bring the Natives to the missions. Once the Natives were there, they were not always allowed to leave. In the missions, the Natives had to work very hard. If they tried to run away, the Spanish soldiers treated them cruelly. Living in the mission was a big change and many of the Natives became ill and died of the new diseases the Spanish brought with them to America.

Central America had three main cultures, the Mayans, the Incas, and the Aztecs. These cultures believed their end was predicted to occur in 1517 and 1519. Spanish conquistadors went to Central

America in 1517 and were in the Native American towns by 1519. They thought of themselves as explorers but the Native Americans must have felt they were invaders. The Spanish killed and conquered the Native Americans. The conquistadors were able to beat all the Native Americans by having a lot of weapons the Native Americans did not have. After the wars, the Natives still did not want to convert to Catholicism until something special happened.

One winter morning in 1531, Juan Diego was on a hill, and a miracle happened.

1524   GIOVANNI VERRAZANO SETS SAIL FOR NEW WORLD   1528   FATHER JUAN JUAREZ APPOINTED BISHOP OF FLORIDA

Suddenly, the Virgin Mary appeared to him as a native pregnant woman. The beautiful sun was behind her, shadowing an outline of her, and she talked to him in the native language he could understand. She said, "Juan, I am the Virgin Mary, the real mother of God." This is important because the Native Americans got together and became Catholic after this miracle. The native Mary is now called Our Lady of Guadalupe. If you're into reading more of this story, turn to the chapter on miracles.

Early Missions

There was a legend of a magic fountain called the Fountain of Youth. It was supposed to make you live forever. It was a legend that led Spain to find Florida. Ponce de Leon landed there on Easter morning. He thought it was beautiful, so he named it Florida, which means, "Land of the Flowers." Ponce de Leon never found the Fountain of Youth because it is not real.

After Ponce de Leon landed in Florida, other people came and the priests tried to convert the Native Americans to Christianity. The Spanish settled in Florida in the fall of 1565, to stop the French from settling. Saint Augustine was the name of their town, which became the main area of the Spanish people. Here they built and started the first parish church, hospital, and seminary in what would be the continental United States. The first bishop to set foot in the United States was Juan de la Cabezas from Cuba. He came over to confirm people. In 1674, seven

1531 OUR LADY OF
GUADALUPE APPEARS

1542 FATHER JUAN PADILLA
BECOMES FIRST MARTYR
IN NORTH AMERICA

America's First Martyr

In the list of 116 martyrs who died in the United States, Father Juan de Padilla leads all of them. He went on an expedition called the Coronado Expedition. Whenever Spain went on an expedition, they would bring a priest. Father de Padilla worked with great success converting Native Americans to be Catholic, but he never returned from one of the expeditions in the southwest. They believe that he was murdered by Native Americans in 1541 because no remains were found.

Professor Woodward speaks to young writers about Catholics coming to America

priests were ordained at the local church. Continually, bishops were assigned to live in Florida for as long as ten years. Within two years, 5,000 converts had surrounded these missions. Hispanic Catholics brought their heritage and culture to Catholicism. One of the Christmas customs Hispanics brought is the Posadas. Posadas means "shelter." During the Posadas, two people dressed as Mary and Joseph go door-to-door asking for shelter.

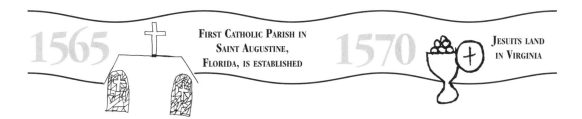

The Colony that Failed

On September 10, 1570, a small Spanish ship came into the harbor, the Bay of the Mother of God, now called Chesapeake Bay, and went up what is now the James River. Near what became Jamestown, nine people got off the ship. They were two Jesuit priests, six Jesuit brothers and a Spanish kid. They were joined by an educated Native American guide. They wanted to convert Native Americans to their religion. They didn't want soldiers to come because they treated Native Americans badly. Soon the nine were met by many mishaps. The Native American Don Luis, who was guiding them, deserted them to live with his tribe. He came back after a while and invited them into his village. This seemed weird, but they went. He swung an ax around killing them all except one of the priests. The priest escaped, but Don Luis found him and put him to death.

More Martyrs

The French began settlements in America at about the same time as the English. They called their first settlements New France. The French were treated better by the Native Americans than the English. In 1524, King Francis I sent Captain Giovanni Verrazano to go explore the New World. He was the first European that sailed into New York harbor. Samuel de Champlain wandered along the Saint

Lawrence River for the first time around 1605. He and two priests settled in Maine. They ministered there until they were attacked and chased away. Champlain said, "It is better to convert one Indian than to conquer an empire."

There were many religious groups in New France. Champlain first asked the Franciscans and then the Jesuits to help him with his missions. He died on Christmas Day in 1635.

The Jesuits became stronger in the northeast area of the United States. The first couple of Jesuit priests came in 1611. They wanted to teach the Native Americans about Jesus, but they found them very hard to deal with. In 1625, Jesuits traveled into what would become New York State. The Iroquois tribe killed the Native Americans that converted to our Catholic faith and all the priests.

Father Isaac Jogues and two missionaries that were not priests, René Goupil and William Couture, went back to Canada in 1642 to get supplies. They were attacked by the Mohawks. When they saw that their Indian friends were captured, the missionaries wanted to be with them. All three of the missionaries were forced to run the gauntlet, which means they had to run all the way back to the camp. While they were running, the Native Americans hit the men with stones. (That would really hurt.) It took the men thirteen days to get to the camp. When they got to camp, the Native Amer-

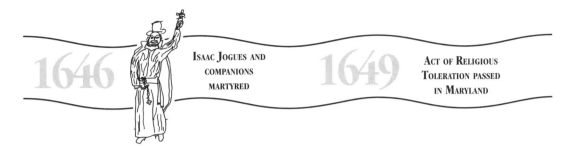

icans kept the men as slaves. Although it was hard, they kept on doing God's work. Some of the Native Americans were so mean that they chopped off Father Jogues' thumbs and pointer fingers, so he could not say Mass. Father was still a slave, but he was happy because he saved souls.

René got axed to death because he made the sign of the cross over a child's head. William was kept as a slave. Father Jogues finally escaped and went to visit the Pope. The Pope said Father Jogues should be able to offer Mass, so the Pope gave Father permission to say Mass with the fingers that he had. Father asked to go back to America. In 1646, Father Jogues went back to the Native Americans who were living in what is now New York State. A young volunteer helper named John de la Lande went with him. When Father Jogues went into one of the houses where he had been a slave, a person tomahawked him in his back and killed him. John was also killed when he went to try and find Father Jogues' body. Father Jogues, René and John have been canonized saints. You can read more about Father Jogues in the saints chapter.

Father Jacques Marquette

Father Jacques Marquette was a Jesuit, too. He was born in France. He came to the Three Rivers Mission in Wisconsin in 1667 to learn about the Native Americans. He founded an American mission, Saint Ignatius, in 1668. Louis Jolliet surprised his friend Father Marquette on December 8, 1672, by arriving at the mission. The king of France wanted to see if the Great River (the Mississippi River) ran into the

1667 FATHER MARQUETTE COMES TO NORTH AMERICA

1672 FATHER MARQUETTE EVANGELIZES ALONG MISSISSIPPI RIVER

Pacific Ocean. The King of France wanted them to start an expedition from Northern Michigan, down the Great River. The beautiful thing about their meeting on December 8 is that this is the feast day of the Immaculate Conception.

The first step of Father Marquette's journey, which started on May 17, 1673, was to stop at a Native American tribe and preach the word of Jesus. In doing so, Father Marquette earned a calumet (a peace pipe), so he would be safe while preaching to other Native American tribes. Father Marquette and his good friend Jolliet made two maps of the Mississippi as they made their way down and back.

Father Jacques Marquette got very sick when he was preaching to the Indians. Some of the Native Americans he converted tried to take him to the mission, but he died in the wilderness. He was only thirty-five years old. His friends took him back to Saint Ignatius Mission where he was buried. He gave his life in 1675 for the Native Americans whom he cared for.

Lydia Longley, First American-Born Nun

Tons of the English people saw the French priests as bad people for two reasons. First of all, the English people were the enemies of the French. And second, the French people were Catholic and most of the English were not. One day in July of 1694, some Native Americans captured all of the Longley family, who were Protestant English settlers. They killed seven out of the ten of them. They took the three children as prisoners. The Native Americans took them to Montreal to be sold as slaves. The little girl, Lydia, was ransomed by a rich Frenchman, Pierre La Bec. Lydia's brother John was forced to live with the Native Americans. The other child died by the road. Lydia became horribly ill. Pierre took her home and cared for her. A few years later in 1697, Lydia converted to the Catholic faith. A year later, 1698, she entered the

order of Notre Dame nuns. Lydia Longley was the first American-born Catholic nun. From Lydia's great example, many joined the Catholic faith.

Father Eusebio Kino

Ever since he was a boy, Father Eusebio Kino wanted to be a missionary in India. He grew up to be a Jesuit priest. Then he asked his superior if he could go to India. The superior said yes, he could get the next ticket to India. Father Kino asked the captain, but the ship was full. Then his superior asked him if he would be a priest in Mexico and Arizona. Father Kino went to America in 1681.

Father Kino was called the "Padre on a Horse" because he

rode a horse for getting around. He taught Native Americans how to grow different crops and raise cattle. Some Native Americans converted to be Catholics. The Apaches were the only Native Americans that refused to listen to Father Kino. The 2,000 miles of paths he traveled on are roads today. Father Kino made fantastic maps. People in other countries even used his maps.

Father Kino sent the first wheat seeds, fruits and vegetables to California. They are still growing there. He started things like watermelons.

Father Kino was dedicating a chapel at Magdalena that was named after Saint Francis Xavier, his favorite saint. Father Kino was singing when he became ill.

1682   La Salle reaches Gulf of Mexico

1727   Ursuline Sisters open Catholic school in New Orleans

When Father Kino was dying, they put two calfskins down for a mattress, two blankets for a cover, and his packsaddle for a pillow. That was his deathbed. He actually died a couple of minutes after midnight on March 15, 1771, at the age of sixty-six.

Blessed Junípero Serra

Father Junípero Serra, a Franciscan, was known throughout Spain for his awesome speeches. Later, Father Serra told the people that all the attention was distracting and he actually wanted to become a missionary in America. So on December 6, 1749, he left and taught at a school in Vera Cruz, Mexico. But, his dream still had not come true. One day a Mexican officer told Father Serra that the Russians were coming to take over California. He told Father how important California was to the Mexicans. Father, who was fifty-six years old, walked to California, and on his way he met some Native Americans and baptized them. Padre Junípero Serra set up Catholic missions, so the Native Americans could learn about the Catholic faith.

Kyle Price

Erin Schmitz

Father Serra was one of the first missionaries. He had leg ulcers and could not even ride horses. He had to walk hundreds of miles between missions on the West Coast. It was said that he baptized 6,000 Native Americans. He would not let anyone hurt the Native Americans. He was called "The Lord's Walker." In fact, he walked 2,400 miles to tell the leaders of the Mexican government that the governor was hurting the Native Americans. The officials were so impressed that they sent another governor with him to replace the bad one. Although the soldiers did not agree with what the priest was doing, they still traveled together.

On August 8, 1784, Father Junípero Serra died while working at the Carmel mission. He was a missionary for thirty-five years. Carmel, San Diego, San Gabriel, Santa Clara, San Luis Obispo, Los Angeles, San Juan Capistrano, San Jose, and San Francisco are nine cities named after nine missions he started. The swallows return to San Juan Capistrano every year on Saint Joseph's Day, March 19. Santa Barbara is the "Queen of the Missions" because it was never destroyed. San Luis Rey is the "King of the Missions." You can still visit these missions today. The state

of California selected a famous California man and woman for their two statues in Washington, D.C. You can see a statue of Father Junípero Serra there as the famous man from California.

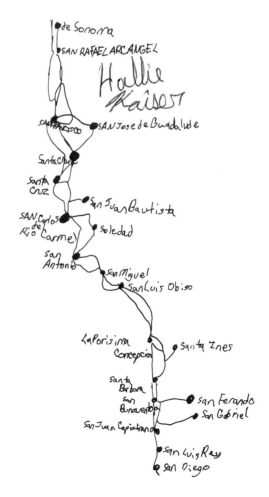

1775   GEORGE WASHINGTON BANS GUY FAWKES DAY CELEBRATIONS

The Declaration of Independence

CHARLES CARROLL SIGNS DECLARATION OF INDEPENDENCE   **1776**

Maryland Colony

In England, the Catholics were treated unfairly. Catholics owned no land so they couldn't build a Catholic church. Some wanted to have freedom, so they sailed on two ships, the Ark and the Dove, to North America. The ships were called that because Noah sent out a dove to find land, and the dove brought back a fresh olive twig to the ark.

The Ark and the Dove set sail on the 22 of November in 1633 from England, to find new land to settle in. On the ships were two Jesuit priests. One of them was Father Andrew White. Also on the ship were builders, blacksmiths and soldiers. During the voyage across the Atlantic, there was a terrible storm, which separated the Dove from the Ark. Since the Dove was lost and the storm was still going on, the Dove went back to England. After the storm the Dove set out again and met up with the Ark in Virginia. They went up the Potomac River and stopped at Saint Clement's Island in March 1634.

England

Right after they landed at Saint Clement's Island, they planted a cross and gave thanks for a safe voyage. There they had the first Mass in an English colony, which was celebrated on March 25, 1634. When Father Andrew reached Maryland, he taught the Native Americans his language.

Lord Baltimore was a Catholic. He was the first to start the Maryland colony. Lord Baltimore allowed the people of Maryland to go to any church they wanted to and allowed them to practice their own religion.

Ten years after the Ark and the Dove ship landed in Maryland, a ship called Reformation carried Puritans over to Maryland. When the ship landed, the Puritans kicked out all the Catholics because they didn't like them. In 1649, the Act of Religious Toleration was passed and the Catholics came back to Maryland. After ten years, the act went downhill until the Revolutionary War.

Other colonies were against Catholicism at this time too. Some colonies had a celebration called Guy Fawkes Day. In England in the year 1605, a small number of Catholic people with Guy Fawkes as their leader planned to blow up the House of Parliament with King James I in it. They were going to blow up the building using the gunpowder in the basement. That's why it was called the "Gunpowder Conspiracy." They were caught and put to death. From then on, some of the people in America celebrated Guy Fawkes Day, making fun of all Catholics. On this day, some people would make a dummy of the Pope, hang it up, and burn it.

America grew quicker than 1,2,3. Soon there were thirteen colonies. The English government ruled America, and Americans didn't like that. The Americans had a meeting called the "Continental Congress" with members from all the colonies. In 1776 they voted to write a document they called the "Declaration of Independence." The paper told about American Freedom in the colonies. In 1787 the Constitution

of the United States was written. It gave Catholics and all other people freedom to practice their religion in America.

When the Revolutionary War came up, the Catholics fought against the English with all people belonging to the other religions. In the Revolution, George Washington banned Guy Fawkes Day forever, because he knew the Catholics were fighting and he didn't want anyone to make fun of them.

We only have room to share about three important Catholics in colonial times. These were John Carroll, Daniel Carroll, and Charles Carroll.

John Carroll

In Europe, John Carroll was called by God to the priesthood. He was ordained in 1761, and came home to Maryland in 1774. He wanted to have a regular church, but they were not allowed in the anti-Catholic English colonies. John was a priest for his mom's large house chapel. He rode on a horse to give the holy sacrament of the Eucharist in Virginia and Maryland. In 1776, Congress chose a committee to go on a mission to Canada. The committee was made up of three people, Daniel Casey, Charles Carroll, and Benjamin Franklin. Franklin reminded the committee that they needed a priest too, to talk to the Archbishop of Montreal.

Charles said, "My cousin is a priest. He can come." They all agreed that he would come. On the way back John Carroll and Benjamin Franklin became good friends.

Then the Pope sent a messenger to Benjamin asking if he knew of any good priests to be a bishop. Of course he said John Carroll. So John Carroll became the first bishop of Baltimore and the first in the whole United States. In 1807, the Catholic population grew so much the Pope made four new dioceses. The Pope also made John Carroll an Archbishop.

Convention. He got to help pick the location for our capital. They put it in Washington, D.C. in the middle of the Northern and Southern states. He personally chose the spot.

Charles Carroll

Charles Carroll was a Catholic in Maryland. Even though he was not allowed to vote, people still respected him. He was elected by Protestants to go to Maryland's legislature. His election stopped the law that Catholics cannot vote. From the day he was born to the day he died, Charles was always a good Catholic citizen.

Religious Orders— Late 1700s and 1800s

The Constitution, which allowed freedom of religion, made a big difference for Catholic Americans. Before it was drawn up in 1787, many people had to lie and say they weren't Catholics. In 1791, the first seminary was Saint Mary's Seminary in Maryland. Sadly enough, any woman who wanted to be a religious sister had to study in Europe before this time.

Daniel Carroll

Daniel Carroll was an important Catholic man in our history. He arrived at his new homeland in America, from England, right before the war for our independence.

Before the war, he was a countryman who was quite smart. He was elected to the Maryland Colonial Congress. After the war, he was one of the representatives from Maryland to the Constitutional

1812 SISTERS OF CHARITY OF NAZARETH FOUNDED IN KENTUCKY

1822 DOMINICAN SISTERS ESTABLISHED IN KENTUCKY

Father Ignatius Matthews of Maryland wrote to his sister in Holland, Mother Bernardina Matthews, telling her that now was the time to come to America to establish an order of nuns. She came, along with three other sisters. The first monastery for nuns in the U.S. was the Carmelite Foundation in Port Tobacco, Maryland, which Mother Bernardina started in 1790.

The Sisters of Charity of Nazareth were founded in 1812, close to Bardstown, Kentucky. Their motto was, "The charity of Christ impels us." The Sisters of Charity's service to their friends and neighbors slowly stretched out of Kentucky and worked its way into twenty other states. The Sisters of Charity's education ministry started in 1814, when

1829 OBLATE SISTERS— FIRST AFRICAN AMERICAN SISTERS—COME TO BALTIMORE

1830 BIRTH OF PATRICK HEALY, WHO WILL BECOME FIRST AFRICAN AMERICAN PRIEST IN U.S.

they opened their first school. In 1832, the sisters started a home for orphans who had been left on the wharves of Louisville, Kentucky.

Nine brave pioneer women were the first Dominican Sisters organized in Kentucky in 1822. Committed to each other and truth, they began a school in the wilderness. Four sisters courageously traveled to Somerset, Ohio, in 1830 to start a congregation. As a community, they are part of the untold story of women's history in America.

The Sisters of Loretto, a religious order founded in Kentucky in 1812, planned from its beginning to open schools. The sisters moved west from Kentucky and opened schools in Missouri (1823) and Kansas (1847). The school in Kansas was for the Osage Native Americans. In 1852, four years after the treaty of Guadalupe Hildalgo, when areas of the southwest became part of the U.S., the sisters were asked to work with the Spanish-speaking children of Santa Fe, New Mexico. Holy women in America helped build the biggest private school system in the world, staffed hospitals, orphanages, old-age homes, and provided home health care for two centuries.

Catholics Immigrate to the United States (1840–1920)

The people who came to America from other countries were known as immigrants. Immigrants brought their Catholic traditions from their own countries. Many Catholic immigrants came to the United States in the late 1800s and early 1900s. Catholics made up almost 25% of the entire United States population by the year 1920.

Europeans came to the U.S. for many reasons including famine, political problems, and financial problems in their

1841 SAINT ROSE PHILIPPINE DUCHESNE BECOMES A MISSIONARY TO KANSAS

1847 SISTERS OF LORETTO OPEN OSAGE INDIAN SCHOOL IN KANSAS

homelands and the desire to spread the Catholic faith. Immigrant Catholics faced problems when they came to the United States. Many people in this country did not like or trust the Catholics. Many immigrants could not speak English and had a hard time fitting into this new land.

In the mid-1840s, Irish Catholics moved to the U.S. because the potato crop failed. This was known as the potato famine. The Irish were among the largest and earliest groups of Catholics to arrive in the United States. Between 1846 and 1851 over a million Irish people came. They

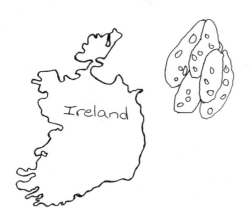

were not welcomed in the U.S. Many of the Irish people were poor and ill. They were picked on and people would not give them jobs. Some of the Protestant people seemed to feel threatened by the Catholics from Ireland. They were afraid that the Catholics would take over, so they burned down some Catholic churches.

When the Irish came, they brought their own holidays like Saint Patrick's Day with them. Tradition tells us that Patrick drove the snakes out of Ireland. (The snakes symbolized the devil.) Legend says that Saint Patrick was on a hill with a wooden staff forcing them into the ocean. The Chapel of Saint Patrick is still at Glastonbury Abbey. To this day, there are no snakes in Ireland. The first Saint Patrick's Day parade was held in Boston in 1737. The idea of the parade crossed back over to Ireland from this country. Saint Patrick's Cathedral was built in New York in 1858. The Irish were leaders in the American Catholic Church in the early 1900s. They were very strict about how people should

 **OVER ONE MILLION IRISH COME TO THE UNITED STATES**

1846–51

practice their faith. Other Catholic immigrants didn't like the strict rules they had made. The Irish immigrants faced anger from some Protestant people and the other immigrant Catholics.

Many poor Italians immigrated to the United States in the early 1900s because they were not allowed to be involved in Italian national politics. There were, however, many hurdles to jump before getting to the U.S. Since many immigrants were very poor, it was quite a challenge to get money for boat passage, food and good water. Still, even with all of the challenges, five million Italians completed the journey to the U.S. When

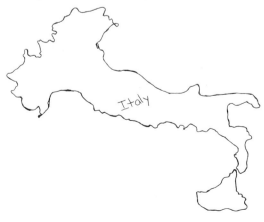

Italy

they arrived in the U.S., most had to live in large cities to find jobs. They also had the problem of having to learn English. At times the Catholics from other European countries were not nice to them, because they didn't understand the Italian culture or language.

POLAND

Many Polish people immigrated to the United States in the 1870s. Some of the first people from Poland went to the German or Irish Catholic churches and schools until they could fund their own. The Polish were among the largest financial contributors to the United States Catholic Church. Fifteen Polish parishes were made by 1870, but by 1930, there were over 800. Their local parishes were the center of their social and political life.

The Polish brought and taught devotion to our Blessed Mother. Two thirds of Polish American children went to the Polish Catholic schools. The classes were usually taught in Polish, and English was taught as a foreign language. The Polish wanted to have a Polish American bishop, but it was not until 1908 that the first Pol-

1854 BIRTH OF FATHER TOLTON, FIRST SLAVE-BORN PRIEST IN UNITED STATES

1858 SAINT PATRICK'S CATHEDRAL BUILT IN NEW YORK CITY

ish American Bishop was ordained. He was the assistant bishop to the archbishop in Chicago.

German Catholics had a big influence on the beginning of the Catholic Church in the U.S. Many settled in the mid-west, in places like Illinois and Minnesota. The Germans wanted to get the German language to be the second language in public schools. When they failed, they started Catholic schools, to

help their culture and language. By 1912, Germans had 346 parishes.

By the late 1800s, the Catholic African American population was approximately 200,000 out of the total African American population of 7 million. Henriette Dellile, Maria Balas, and Elizabeth Lange were among the important people who helped African American Catholics. Maria Balas and Elizabeth Lange were the first two African American nuns. They formed the Oblate Sisters of Providence. They taught African American children who could not attend public schools. Henriette Dellile was born in New Orleans in 1813. Henriette joined with some other women. They prayed and helped the poor. Eventually they bought a house, where they gave food and clothing to African Americans. They taught African Americans too. In 1852, Henriette and some of her friends started their own group of sisters. They were

IMMIGRATION TO THE U.S.   1820-1860

Country of Origin	Number	Main Destinations
IRELAND	2,100,000	large cities especially in Northeast
ENGLAND	750,000	Northeast and GREAT LAKES area
GERMANY	1,700,000	farms in upper mississippi and Ohio
FRANCE	50,000	scattered
SWITZERLAND	40,000	farms in Wisconsin
NETHERLANDS	20,000	NEW YORK

called the Sisters of the Holy Family. She helped people with yellow fever and continued to help the poor. Sister Henriette was ill for a long time and died after about ten years in 1862.

Catholic schools were about the only place African American children could get an education. By the late 1800s, there were twenty churches each with their own school and sixty-five other schools that taught African American Catholics.

Father Patrick Healy, born in 1830, of an Irish father, and an African American mother, was the first U.S.-born African American priest. This great man became president of Georgetown University in 1868.

Born in 1854, Father Tolton was the first slave-born priest in the U.S. Father Tolton served in Quincy, Illinois and later in Chicago. Today there are about fourteen African American bishops in the United States.

In the 1920s the Irish and Italians, who were first disliked when they arrived in America, became respected as model Catholic citizens. The Protestants and Catholics joined bonds while fighting side by side in World War I. Catholics proved they were real Americans when they helped fight in the wars.

James Cardinal Gibbons

Although many European Catholics had to face discrimination and hatred when they came to the U.S., some people did try to help them. James Gibbons was one of these. He was the ninth Archbishop of Baltimore, Maryland. He worked to convince Americans that it was possible for Catholics to be good American citizens.

There were times when some of the Catholic immigrants fought among themselves. Archbishop Gibbons was known to preach on the importance of unity and remind each group that we are all one body in Christ. In 1884, Gibbons was the leader of a gathering of United States Bishops that met in Baltimore. They came together to talk about the problems that many Catholics faced in America. They set up the parish school system and decided to have a catechism to be taught to all American Catholic children. Many people know this as the Baltimore catechism. Archbishop Gibbons worked very

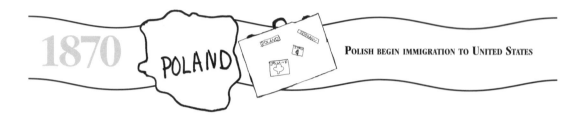

hard for the Catholic people of Baltimore, and he was made a cardinal for all his great work.

The Catholic School System

The Catholic school system in America has a cool history. The Ursuline Sisters started the first Catholic school of New Orleans back in 1727. They wanted to begin these schools so that Catholic children could learn about their faith during the school day. By 1884, four parishes out of every ten had a Catholic school. Over 800,000 students went to Catholic schools by 1900. Now the United States Catholic school system is the largest private school system in the world. Some important people that helped set up the school system were Saint John Neumann and Saint Elizabeth Ann Seton. You can read about them in the chapter about saints.

Boys' Town

Father Flanagan was known in the city of Omaha as the tall and skinny young priest from Saint Patrick's Church who ran a workmen's hotel for down and out men. Father Flanagan was an assistant pastor. He wanted to help poor and homeless boys. He was given permission to raise money to start a home for boys. On December 12, 1917, Father Flanagan opened a home for twelve boys. This was

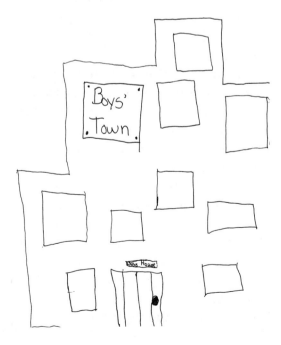

the beginning of Boys' Town. Eventually, Girls' Town would be started for poor and homeless girls. Today you can still visit this place in Omaha, Nebraska.

Modern Immigration

The Mexican-American War was from 1846 to 1848. When the war was over, the Americans won, leaving thousands of Mexicans in the new American territory. After the war, there were still some hard feelings. The original Mexican priests were replaced with European priests.

In the 1930s, Mexicans immigrated to the U.S. to be farm laborers, so they could get money. By 1940, there were one million Mexican Americans in Los Angeles. Many became American citizens.

Between 1940 to 1960, there were almost 300,000 Puerto Ricans who immigrated to the New York area. In the 1970s, they were a big part of the cursillo movement, which means, "little course." This means that they wanted Jesus to be an everyday part of their lives.

1927 — **BIRTH OF CESAR CHAVEZ**   1928 — **DOROTHY DAY BECOMES A CATHOLIC**

In the 1960s, Cuban immigrants came to the United States. They left Cuba after the Communist government took over. The Communists did not allow Catholics to worship. Most of the immigrants settled in Florida. Many Cubans sent their children to the United States, because they could not afford to send the whole family. Some orphanages were started for the Cuban immigrants.

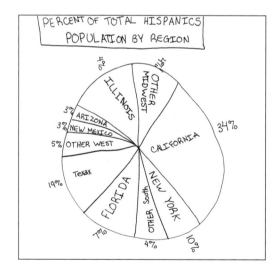

Nationwide, 25% of all Catholics are Hispanic. Many parishes all over the United States have Spanish Masses. Mexican American vocations are encouraged. Hispanic customs, such as the feast of Our Lady of Guadalupe, Posadas and Epiphany are celebrated in many parishes.

Hispanics that are important in the Catholic faith today include such people as Bishop Roberto Gonzalez. He was born in Elizabeth, New Jersey. He was one of the youngest priests to be ordained a bishop. He was only thirty-eight years old and became a bishop in 1988. His hero is actually his dad. His grandmother, from Puerto Rico, also was important in his life. She taught him and his brothers and sisters to always serve God and take care of their family's graves.

Filipino immigrants included scholars, laborers, soldiers, professional businessmen, and later whole families. Filipinos emphasize rites, ceremonies, and devotional practices in the practice of their Catholic faith. The Flores de Mayo is a devotional prayer to Mary. They also

celebrate the feast of Lorenzo Ruiz, who was the first Filipino martyr. They have large churches, but family devotions are very important. There are 300 Filipino priests, brothers, and deacons, and there are 200 nuns in the United States. The Filipino community stresses religious education for their children.

The population of Asian and Pacific Islanders in the U. S. has doubled between 1980 and 1990. Some Asian Americans still live in a "cultural no-man's land." For these people "home is roots, relationships, and family. A meal is a time for sitting down and sharing family stories." New immigrants are often thought of as foreigners in America. But, when they visit their homeland, they are thought of as Americans. Unfortunately, it is sometimes the same in the Church. Vietnamese people are extremely proud of their history of suffering for the faith. In 1988, Pope John Paul II canonized 117 Vietnamese martyrs. Nowadays, Asian Americans are encouraging vocations to the priesthood and religious life for their children.

CHINA

LAOS

THAILAND

CAMBODIA

VIET NAM

MALAYSIA

VIET NAM

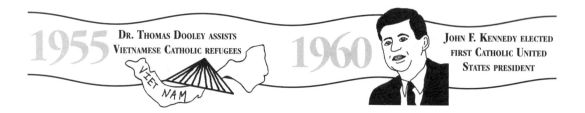

1955 — DR. THOMAS DOOLEY ASSISTS VIETNAMESE CATHOLIC REFUGEES

VIET NAM

1960 — JOHN F. KENNEDY ELECTED FIRST CATHOLIC UNITED STATES PRESIDENT

Popes, Starting from Vatican II

In 1959, **Pope John XXIII** invited the world's bishops to gather in Rome for a Council to address how the Church might proclaim the Gospel to a changing world. Pope John XXIII had big goals too. He asked for nothing less than a new Pentecost to sweep the Church and the world. He knew God worked wonders through his people. People all over the world were sad when this well-loved Pope died in 1963.

The Council Pope John wanted began in 1962. It was called the Vatican Council II. **Pope Paul VI** (1963–78) had to take

A young author meets the Pope!

Photo courtesy of the Yakes family

Photo credit: James Baca

Pope John Paul II at 1993 World Youth Day in Denver

over the Vatican Council II and he opened a bond with other Christians and the modern world. He made these changes slowly and steadily. He also knew that the Catholic Church must be a part of the modern world. In 1965, he met with President Johnson to discuss ways of ending the Vietnam War.

After Vatican II, there were some big differences that Catholics noticed and liked. Before Vatican II the altar was against the church wall and the priest's back was all the people could see during Mass. But today the altar is moved forward and the priest faces the people. Before Vatican II, most Catholics were not allowed to go up near the altar, unless there was a special reason, like being an altar server or getting married. Today everyone can go there. Kids can even do the readings during Mass! Did you know that all Masses in the United States used to be said in Latin? After Vatican II, the Mass is said in whatever language is spoken in the community. In the U.S., Mass can be in many languages, such as Spanish, Vietnamese, Korean, and English.

1975 ELIZABETH ANN SETON—
FIRST UNITED STATES-BORN
SAINT—CANONIZED

1978 JOHN PAUL II
BECOMES POPE

*Deacon Clarence McDavid points out the Gospel
he read at the Pope's World Youth Day Mass*

of illness, the Pope became healthy again. He really believes what Jesus said about spreading the Gospel to the whole world. Pope John Paul II has traveled to many places in Africa, North and South America, Europe, and Asia. World Youth Day is always a favorite event for the Pope. He wants the young people of the world to keep Jesus in their lives all the time. He celebrated World Youth Day in Denver, Colorado in 1993. Pope John Paul II has also visited many other American and Canadian cities at different times.

John Paul II is our present Pope. His birth name was Karol Wojtyla. He is Polish and is the first non-Italian Pope in 455 years. Cardinal Wojtyla became Pope on October 16, 1978. In 1981, he got shot while greeting the crowds in Saint Peter's Square. After many months

1993

Some Famous Twentieth Century American Catholics

Photo credit: CNS

Cesar Chavez

Cesar Chavez was born on March 31, 1927, near Yuma, Arizona. He was the second of six children. Cesar began school at age seven. It was hard because he only spoke Spanish. In the 1930s, his dad lost his business because of the Great Depression. They moved to California in search of work. After attending more than thirty schools he quit and began working full time. Chavez started a strike protesting low wages. It wasn't successful. He led two more protests in his life that were successful. Chavez began the United Farm Workers' Union. He died on April 23, 1993.

Dorothy Day spent her early life without a purpose. In 1928, Dorothy became a Catholic. Then she became a non-stop worker for justice with a love for the poor. She spoke out against war and went to jail for her beliefs. She started a newspaper called "The Catholic Worker." She sold it for a penny apiece and it's still sold for that much today! Dorothy Day said: "God made things to be easier than we have made them. Eternal life begins now. And love makes all things easy." Before Dorothy Day died in 1980, many people called her a saint.

Photo credit: CNS

Dorothy Day

2000   KATHARINE DREXEL CANONIZED—SECOND U.S.-BORN SAINT

Bishop Fulton J. Sheen

Al Smith

Bishop Fulton J. Sheen was the first clergyman to have a regular radio and TV show. His show "Life is Worth Living" was one of the most popular shows of the 1950s. Sheen said, "Little did I know that it would be given to me to address a greater audience in a half an hour than Saint Paul in all the years of his missionary life."

Al Smith, the Catholic governor of New York, ran for the presidency in 1928. He did not win because many people were against him because he was a Catholic. However, in 1960 a Catholic did win the presidency of the United States. **John F. Kennedy** was the first Catholic elected to the office. Many people were afraid to

have a Catholic president because they thought the Pope would tell the president what to do. After the people saw the

John F. Kennedy

2001 DEDICATION OF POPE JOHN PAUL II CULTURAL CENTER IN WASHINGTON, D.C.

president and his family going to Mass on Sundays and seeing bishops and cardinals on TV, many were not afraid of Catholics anymore. By being a Catholic president, he changed some Americans' point of view of our religion.

On March 22, 2001, President George W. Bush had this to say when he spoke at the dedication of the John Paul II Cultural Center, a new museum and interactive learning center, in Washington, D.C. "The center we dedicate today celebrates the Pope's message, its comfort and its challenge. This place stands for the dignity of the human person, the value of every life and the splendor of truth. And, above all, it stands, in the Pope's own words, for the 'joy of faith in a troubled world'…. The Pope bears the message our world needs to hear."

The Catholic faith is continuing to grow and prosper across our great country.

This is a small part of the wonderful history of our faith in America. We hope you'll research and study to learn more!

Photo credit: CNS

John Paul II Cultural Center

SAINTS AND SAINTLY PEOPLE

A saint is someone who really cares.
A saint is someone who treats you fair.
A saint is someone who cares for you and me.
A saint wants us to be all we can be.

Saints are cool! They are good people. They are very special friends of God. Because of the holy lives they lead, the Catholic Church chooses to recognize them as saints.

A saint usually touches the lives of many people. These people get together and talk about making a person a saint. In the early Church, the first saints were martyrs and were chosen to be saints by popular vote.

In the 10th century, the Catholic Church made some official rules about canonization. The Pope usually canonizes people in Rome. Canonization means the Church recognizes saints as special people and puts them on a list called the Canon of Saints. The process has three steps. Each step has a title. The very first step, VENERABLE, means

someone is worthy of respect. Next, BLESSED means a person has one miracle attached to his or her name. Finally, SAINT means that a person has been canonized and that two miracles have been linked to his or her name. When a miracle is linked to a saint, it is proof that that person is in heaven and is praying for us.

Listening to a presentation on the saints

Mary

Our Blessed Mother Mary has a very honored place in the Catholic Church. Some people call Mary the Queen of All Saints. She is the greatest of all saints because she is Jesus' mother. At the very second God created Mary, he made her very special. He gave her a very pure soul, and she remained without sin all her life. God's plan for her was to become the Mother of God, so she had to have no sin in her. Because of this, we call Mary the Immaculate Conception.

We don't know a lot about Mary's childhood. Tradition tells us that her parents' names were Saint Anne and Saint Joachim. She was raised in a faithful Jewish family. She was dedicated to God and was taught about the Scriptures.

We pray to Mary because she gives our prayers directly to God. Jesus is God's Son and Mary's Son. Jesus wants us to pray to Mary, too, since he gave her to us as our Heavenly Mother. We can always feel really good going to Mary in prayer, because she loves and cares for us so much. Mary is so kind, helpful and generous. She really wants to help us. Mary always leads us to Jesus. A very special prayer we pray to Mary is called the rosary. As we pray Our Fathers and Hail Marys on the beads, we think about the different events in Jesus' and Mary's lives.

We are blessed to have Mary as the Patroness of the United States, under the title of the Immaculate Conception. We love being under her special care! In Washington, D.C. there is a beautiful church called the Basilica of the Immaculate Conception. We hope you can visit it sometime!

Saint Frances Xavier Cabrini

Photo credit: CNS

Saint Frances Xavier Cabrini (1850–1917)

Canonized: 1946
Feast Day: November 13

Maria Francesca Cabrini was born in Italy to a very holy family. Now let us tell you that there were thirteen children in her family. There were seven boys and six girls. Maria was in love with the Sacred Heart of Jesus. Who wouldn't be?

Maria always wanted to be a missionary to China. When she was a young girl, she made a paper boat and filled it with violets. She put it in the water and it started to float away. She hoped it was going to China. Because she was leaning over the riverbank, she fell into the water and she couldn't save herself. It was cold. She felt strong arms lift her up and put her on the shore. When she looked around, she found no one there. She decided her rescuer was her Guardian Angel.

Maria always wanted to be a nun. She attempted to become a nun on two occasions, but both times she was rejected because of her poor health. Each time there were pebbles in her path, but God opened heaven and he moved those pebbles. When Maria was thirty years old she officially began a religious order called the Missionaries of the Sacred Heart of Jesus. Then she changed her name to Frances Xavier. She chose that name in honor of Saint Francis Xavier, because he was a missionary to China, and he was her favorite saint.

In 1889, Pope Leo XIII sent Mother Cabrini west rather than east. She went to New York City to work with the many Italian immigrants. In her lifetime, she traveled across the ocean twenty-eight times. This was very hard because she was afraid of the water. She opened places for people who had no place to live. She began opening orphanages, schools, hospitals and convents throughout the United States and other parts of the world during the next twenty-seven years.

While in Colorado, Mother Cabrini helped the coal miners and their families. She also planned to start a special summer camp for the orphaned children. Mother and fifteen children traveled in a wagon one day to the bottom of a big mountain. They got out and climbed to the top. There was a problem. There was no water, and it would take a day and a half to haul water from Denver.

Mother Cabrini gathered the children around and told them to collect white rocks. They made the shape of a heart with a cross at the bottom, just like the Sacred Heart of Jesus.

Mother Cabrini tapped on a rock because Jesus told her to. Then she moved the rock. The children started to dig. There was a spring. The water gushed out of the ground! "Yea! We have water!" they shouted. They all took a drink. Today, you can visit the Shrine of Mother Cabrini and have a drink of this water, too.

Mother Cabrini Shrine is located in Golden, Colorado, near exit 252 of Interstate 70. The shrine used to be an orphanage. It is a very beautiful, peaceful, prayerful place. You get lots of exercise because there are piles of steps. You can stop to pray at the fourteen Stations of the Cross or the fifteen decades of the rosary. After making this journey, you're at the top of the world near a huge statue of the Sacred Heart of Jesus.

At the bottom of the hill there is a chapel. Jesus is on the wall behind the altar in colorful cutglass. In the room by the chapel, there are several large stained glass windows that tell the story of the life of Mother Cabrini and her canonization. She became the first American saint. Downstairs there is a display of Mother Cabrini's bedroom with a quilt that Mother Cabrini made with her own hands. One of the patches on the quilt says, "Peace to all".

Saint Katharine Drexel
(1858–1955)

Canonized: 2000
Feast Day: March 3

Saint Katharine Drexel

The Drexel family, very rich people, shared the happy news of Katharine's birth with the rest of Philadelphia on a rainy November day in 1858. Then sadness struck the family. A few days after Katharine's birth, her mother passed away.

Katharine's father got remarried, and Katharine was a happy child. She only wanted one thing and that was to help the poor. When Katharine was twelve, her family opened their big mansion to the poor three times a week. Katharine devoted her life to God. When her stepmother got sick with cancer, Katharine took care of her until she died.

One day Katharine visited Pope Leo XIII, because of her concern about the state of the American Indians. She asked the Pope to send more missionaries to Wyoming. Pope Leo XIII suggested that Katharine herself become a missionary. To learn how to live as a religious sister, Katharine joined the Sisters of Mercy and took the name Sister Mary Katharine.

Then in 1891, Sister Mary Katharine started a new religious order called the Sisters of the Blessed Sacrament. From then on she was called Mother Mary Katharine. The Sisters of the Blessed Sacrament were dedicated to sharing the Gospel with the Native Americans and African Americans. In 1894, Mother Mary Katharine founded the first mission school in Santa Fe, New Mexico. With the help of her sisters, Mother Katharine was able to start fifty missions, a system of Catholic schools for African Americans, forty mission centers, twenty-three rural schools and Xavier University for African Americans in the United States.

One night in 1922 in Beaumont, Texas, a note was left on the door where the Sisters of the Blessed Sacrament had just opened their new school. The note had a threat saying that if the school did not close its doors to people of color, the school would be destroyed. The note was signed KKK (Ku Klux Klan). Katharine prayed to God to protect her and the other people within the building. A few days later a violent thunderstorm started. Suddenly, several bolts of lighting struck the building that served as the Klan's headquarters and destroyed it. That was when Mother Katharine's prayer was answered and their school was safe.

When Mother Mary Katharine Drexel was seventy-seven, a heart attack forced her to retire. She spent the last nineteen years of her life praying for everyone. Mother Katharine showed us that one lady, with God on her side, can make the world a better place. We now call her Saint Katharine Drexel. She was canonized in the year 2000.

Young authors sharing what they've learned about the saints

Saint Philippine Duchesne (1769–1850)

Canonized: 1988
Feast Day: November 18

Saint Philippine Duchesne was born in France. When she was twelve years old, she went to a boarding school run by the Visitation nuns. When she was eighteen years old, she entered the Visitation convent and chose the name Rose. Sadly, the French Revolution took place in 1789, and her convent was closed. When the government changed its mind, Philippine tried to reopen her old convent by buying it with her own money. The other nuns were not interested, so Philippine joined the Society of the Sacred Heart of Jesus.

Rose Philippine wanted to take the Gospel to the Indians. She wanted to go to America. It took her a long time to get permission. In 1818, at the age of forty-nine, she set sail for America with several sisters of the Society of the Sacred Heart. They landed in Saint Louis and started several schools in Missouri.

Finally, in 1841, when Mother Philippine Duchesne was seventy-two, she and four other nuns became missionaries to the Potowatomi Indians in Kansas. The language was too difficult for Mother Duchesne, so she spent most of the time praying to ask God to help the missions. The Indians called her "The woman who prays always."

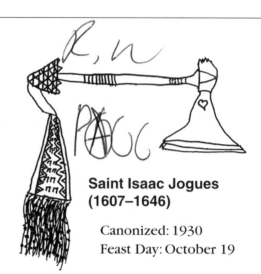

Saint Isaac Jogues (1607–1646)

Canonized: 1930
Feast Day: October 19

One day Father Isaac Jogues was traveling in canoes with two Frenchmen and a ton of Huron Indians. They were in what is now New York State. Suddenly, they heard war cries coming from the shore. As bullets came screaming over their heads, Father Jogues asked if he could baptize Chief Ahatsistari. Chief Ahatsistari agreed and took the baptismal name Eustace. Father Jogues took water from the river and blessed it. Then he baptized Eustace with it.

The Iroquois captured Father Jogues, took him prisoner and tortured him. The Indians forced the captives to run all the way back to the camp. It took thirteen days to get to the camp. While the captives were running, the Indians hit the men with stones. When they got to camp, the Indians kept the men as slaves. During this time of slavery, one man got axed to death because the Indians saw him make the sign of the cross over a child's head. Father Jogues prayed and called the Indians "the narrow road to Heaven." The Indians stretched Father Jogues' body over a dirt floor and staked his arms and legs to the ground. They covered his body with hot coals and ashes. Then the Iroquois took him from village to village and in each village, they tortured him again. The Iroquois used their teeth to bite off Father Jogues' thumb and pointer finger and then put a sword through his hands so he could not say Mass. As the Indians took him through the woods Father Jogues would carve the sign of the cross and the name "Jesus" on the trees. Throughout all the torture, Father tried to share the good news of Jesus with the

Indians, but they would not listen.

Finally, Father Jogues escaped. He returned on a ship to France. Then he went to Rome to see the Pope. He asked if it would be all right for him to celebrate Mass, even if he was not able to hold his badly injured hands in the correct way. Father Isaac Jogues got the permission from the Pope. In 1646, Father returned to North America. He was killed by an Iroquois tomahawk as he was entering a Mohawk longhouse where he had been invited for dinner.

Saint John Neumann (1811–1860)

Canonized: 1977
Feast Day: January 5

John Neumann was born in Bohemia, where he studied to become a priest. When it came time for him to be ordained, though, his bishop had stopped all ordinations. There were just too many priests! This is hard to believe—too many priests. John wrote to the bishops in America. He was invited to come to New York City, and he was ordained.

Father John Neumann knew how to speak seven languages including English,

Bohemian, Spanish, French, Italian, Dutch and Gaelic. This helped him understand people in the confessional. He had a special love for children. He wrote and taught catechism. He kept his pockets full of candy, which he gave children when they learned their catechism.

In 1852, Father Neumann was appointed Bishop of Philadelphia. At that time, there were two Catholic schools in the city. By the time he died just eight years later, there were 100 Catholic schools! Bishop John Neumann is also given credit for bringing the Forty Hours Devotion to parishes in America. This devotion encourages people to take turns praying in front of the Blessed Sacrament for forty hours.

As a Redemptorist, Bishop Neumann had the vow of poverty. He owned only one habit and one pair of shoes. When he died, he was dressed in new clothes for his journey to heaven. It brought smiles to some of the people who passed by his coffin.

Bishop John Neumann had a strong devotion to Saint Anthony of Padua. He once lost something important and prayed to Saint Anthony to help him find it. We believe Bishop John Neumann could be responsible for the prayer to Saint Anthony:

"Dear Saint Anthony,
please look around.
Something has been lost
that must be found."

Bishop Neumann was beatified on October 13, 1963 and named a saint on July 19, 1977. John Neumann was the first American bishop to be canonized a saint.

Saint Elizabeth Ann Seton

Saint Elizabeth Ann Seton (1774–1821)

Canonized: 1975
Feast Day: January 4

Elizabeth Seton was a convert to Catholicism. She grew up in New York. She became the first American-born saint by living a life of charity and fidelity. Elizabeth's father was a doctor who helped the poor and not the rich. Through his good work with the poor, his children learned how to help others.

Elizabeth's early years were painful, hard and full of tragedy. When she was three, her mother died. When she was four, her sister Catherine died. She didn't cry when Catherine died because she knew she was in heaven with her mom.

A few years later Elizabeth's father re-married a very religious woman of the Protestant faith. When Elizabeth was young, she enjoyed helping her step-mother teach her younger siblings their prayers. They took food to the sick and poor near her home.

At the age of eighteen, she met William Seton, a wealthy shipbuilder. They got married and had five children. William became sick with tuberculosis and was sent to Italy to recover. He died. During her visit to Italy, Elizabeth found a new faith, the Catholic faith. After she re-turned home to New York, she became a Catholic.

One of the first things Elizabeth did after returning home was to get a job as a teacher. Her friends and family wouldn't help support Elizabeth and her children because she had become a Catholic. Some people even discouraged parents from sending their children to the school where Elizabeth was teaching. And so the school was shut down.

This didn't stop Elizabeth's dream. One year later, she traveled to Baltimore and with the permission of Bishop John Carroll, she started the first Catholic parish school.

Throughout Elizabeth's life, she accomplished many things. She established a Catholic orphanage and the religious order now known as the Sisters of Charity.

Venerable Pierre Toussaint (year of birth unknown–1853)

Declared Venerable: 1996

"He radiated a most serene and joyful faith, nourished daily by the Eucharist and visits to the Blessed Sacrament." These are the words Pope John Paul II said about Pierre Toussaint.

What do you know about the man who could become the first African American saint? His name is Pierre Toussaint. His birth date is unknown, but we do know that he was born a slave on the island of Haiti. His family and master were devout

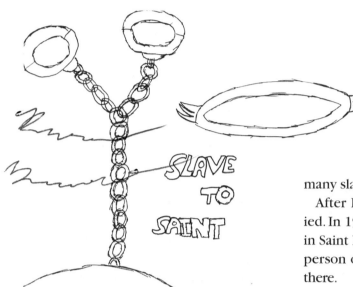

Catholics and loved God very much. When Pierre was young, his master allowed him to learn to read and write.

Pierre's master took him to New York City because of the uprisings in Haiti. His master helped Pierre become a hairdresser. Pierre earned a lot of money. He gave practically all of his money to help other people and hardly thought of himself. He was even able to help his master's wife when she became poor. He helped her until her death. She offered Pierre freedom, but he refused so he could take care of her.

Pierre worked sixteen hours a day. He attended Mass every morning for sixty years. When he wasn't working, he was helping people. He had to walk everywhere. Pierre wasn't allowed to ride in carriages, because he was black. He help-ed African Americans as well as other people. He helped the victims of the plague (a contagious disease) by providing them with comfort and prayers. Pierre founded the first black Catholic school in New York. He also helped many slaves get their freedom.

After Pierre's death his body was buried. In 1990 it was placed under the altar in Saint Patrick's Cathedral. He is the first person other than a bishop to be buried there.

If you have a serious health problem, you might pray to Pierre Toussaint for help. He needs a couple of miracles to become a saint, and you could be one of them. Although he has not been named a saint yet, we know he will be, because of his Christ-like life. He is already a saint in all of our hearts.

Young author getting ideas on paper

Blessed Junípero Serra (1713–1784)

Beatified: 1988
Feast Day: July 1

Miguel Joseph Serra was born in the town of Petra, Majorca, Spain. At age seventeen, he joined the Franciscan Order. In 1730, he received his habit and took the name of Junípero (Jester of God). Junípero had been the name of one of Saint Francis of Assisi's companions. Father Junípero Serra was ordained in 1737.

In 1750, Father Junípero landed in Mexico. He had to travel 240 miles to Mexico City on foot. As he was traveling, he was bitten by an insect. The bite turned into an infection, which left him lame and in lots of pain for the rest of his life.

Father established nine missions in what later became the United States of America. The names of these missions were: San Antonio, San Diego, San Gabriel, San Luis Obispo, San Francisco, San Juan Capistrano, Santa Clara, San Buenaventura and Carmel. Cities in California still have these names. Father Junípero Serra is called the Apostle of California even today.

Father Junípero converted thousands of Na-

tive Americans to the Catholic faith. His motto was, "Always look forward and never look back."

Blessed Kateri Tekakwitha (1656–1680)

Beatified: 1980
Feast Day: July 14

This is a story about a young girl named Kateri Tekakwitha, Lily of the Mohawks, who was born in 1656 in an Indian village near where the town of Auriesville, New York is today. Kateri had smallpox when she was four years old. It left her partially blind with scars on her face. Tekakwitha means "she who pushes with her hands." (Since Kateri couldn't

see well, she had to feel around a lot.) Kateri's mother was a Christian Algonquin who was captured by the Mohawks and made into a slave. Her father was a Mohawk chief. When he saw how beautiful Kateri's mother was, he saved her from slavery.

Kateri's parents and brother died of smallpox when she was only four years old. Her aunts and an uncle adopted Kateri. Her uncle became Chief of the Turtle Clan.

When Kateri was eighteen the Jesuit missionaries spent three days in the lodge of Tekakwitha's uncle. Her family did not want Kateri to be a Christian and wanted her to marry. Kateri totally DID NOT want to marry, even though she was teased and made fun of for her decision. She wanted to offer her life to God and strongly believed in her faith. From the missionaries Kateri accepted knowledge of Christianity. When she was about twenty years old, she was baptized. Fearing for her life, she went to the Indian Christian community of Mission du Sault in Canada.

Blessed Kateri Tekakwitha lived a life dedicated to prayer and cared for the sick and aging. Every morning, even in the bitterest winter, she stood at the chapel door until it opened at 4:00 A.M. and she stayed until after the last Mass.

During the last year of her life on earth, she received mystical gifts and was loved by the Native Americans. While Kateri was dying the priest saw that her scars had gone away and he heard her last words, "Jesus, I love YOU."

Kateri Tekakwitha is the first Native American to be declared Blessed. Kateri was responsible for a lot of the growth of Native American Catholic churches in the United States and Canada.

Mother Teresa

Mother Teresa of Calcutta (1910–1997)

Mother Teresa has not been canonized a saint yet, and she did not live in the United States. But we think she is a very

Sarah Lorenz

saintly person, and she visited our country many times. That's why we are putting her story here.

One day a reporter saw Mother Teresa picking little bugs out of a person's open wounds with her bare hands. The reporter said, "I couldn't do that for a million dollars." Mother Teresa told him, "I couldn't do it for a million dollars either, but I could do it for the love of Christ!" Mother Teresa dedicated her life to helping the poor, sick, and elderly. She looked for sick and dying people to help them and she built shelters for them. Children were always so special to Mother Teresa because she saw in them the image of God, and sometimes they were the ones who needed her most.

The very first time Mother Teresa did something for the poor was when she found a woman lying on the street half eaten by rats. She took her to the hospital, but they could do nothing for her. Mother Teresa refused to go home until something was done for the woman. She cared so much about her.

MOTHER TERESA

Because of the great need to help the poor, Pope Paul VI gave Mother Teresa permission to expand missions all over the world. Mother opened schools and homes for the poor and abandoned children, and helped the sick and suffering people in many different countries. Mother Teresa even opened many missions in the United States. One of these missions is in Denver, Colorado. It is called Seton House. The sisters here take care of men who are sick with AIDS.

Mother Teresa has made a beautiful difference in the lives of so many people throughout the world. One night, a boy came to Mother Teresa's house. He yelled, "My mom doesn't want me. My dad doesn't want me. What about you? Do you want me?" Mother Teresa said, "Yes, my child, I do want you." Then Mother let him in and made him a part of her and her sisters' family.

There was another time when Mother Teresa was walking down the street. Some children were walking with her. She sat down under a tree and started teaching the children about important things like using soap and water. And then she rewarded them with soap bars!

Mother Teresa's love didn't stop with people either. There was a priest who had a dog. Every time he visited a certain school, the dog would have to stay outside because the sister superior of the school wouldn't let the dog in. One day

Mother Teresa came to this school to celebrate its twenty-fifth anniversary. The sisters had invited the priest, but not his dog. While everyone was having some tea inside, the priest's dog quietly crept into the school and went right up to Mother Teresa. The angry sister superior started to shoo the dog away, but Mother Teresa started giving it hugs and kisses. From then on, whenever the priest came to visit, the dog was always let in, because Mother Teresa had blessed it!

Authors give this chapter a final look

Mother Teresa won the Nobel Peace Prize in 1979 and gave all the money to the poor. We would like to end this story of Mother Teresa by giving her an award from us! It is a trophy with hearts on it, filled with our love and thanks to her for all the beautiful things she has done for God and for our world.

God Calls All of Us to Be Saints

How can we become saints? We begin by having a relationship with God. We need to love one another as Jesus loved us. This is the Commandment of Love. We need to keep the Ten Commandments that God gave to Moses. We need to do unto others as we would have them do unto us. This is the Golden Rule. We need to receive the sacraments. It is especially important that we receive the two sacraments of Reconciliation and Holy Eucharist often. They make us strong.

We also need to pray to God and we need to ask the saints to pray to God for us. We do not worship saints. We worship God only, in the Blessed Trinity. We pray to God through the saints. This is called intercessory prayer. It is like asking your mom to plead with your father for a special privilege. We need to ask our patron saints, those given to us in our baptismal names and those we choose for Confirmation, to look after us for all of our lives.

GROWING UP CATHOLIC

Growing up in the Catholic faith,
We learn Bible stories like Adam and Eve and the snake.
We go to Mass on Sunday, it's the greatest way to pray.
We learn about new life, toward heaven we trod.
We learn all about Jesus, and we love God!

It is awesome to grow up Catholic and learn about Jesus through our beautiful faith. There are many places and ways to learn about the beliefs and practices of the Catholic religion. Now we want to share another way: this book was written to share the beauty of our Catholic journey. We will take you through the sacra-

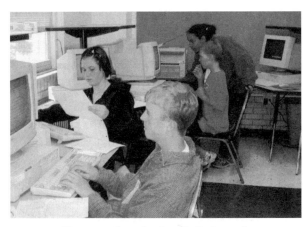

Young authors keying in their work

ments and even a funeral, because dying isn't bad if you have grown up loving God and trying to please him.

For most Catholics, the experience of their faith begins before they are able to speak or act for themselves, at their baptism. Here, the children become members of the Church, and their parents promise to begin teaching their children to develop their beliefs, and learn about God and Jesus at church.

Luke and James, two boys who helped write this chapter, both get dressed up and go to church every Sunday with their families. Before James was old enough to receive the Eucharist, he would watch his parents and all the other people go to Communion. He was excited about getting older so he could receive the Body and Blood of Christ too. "I couldn't wait to be in second grade because Mom said that was when I would receive this sacrament." Luke knew it was important to be quiet and listen to the Gospel readings. He also liked holding hands during the Our Father prayer. "I knew that prayer," Luke explains, "and so then I felt really special."

As Catholic parents continue to raise their children in the faith, they begin teaching them about the Mass, and helping them to learn prayers like the Our Father, the Hail Mary, the Glory Be, the Act of Contrition, and the prayer before meals. Many young Catholics also spend time praying to God in both happy times and times of need. Sometimes they pray alone and at other times they gather as a family to offer special prayers. We pray before bed each night and thank God for everything. Sometimes we hear Bible stories. These experiences help us learn about how important it is to pray, talk, and listen to God, throughout our life.

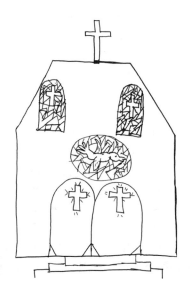

Luke says, "In my family we go to church every Sunday. We also have special holiday celebrations which include going to Mass together. On Christmas Day we go to remember Jesus' birth, and on Easter Sunday we celebrate Jesus' resurrection, the day Jesus rose from the dead." Baylen, another author, also remembers sitting down with her family around Christmas and Easter to watch religious shows and movies on television. "This was a fun way for me to learn about Jesus' birth and crucifixion."

As their children get older many parents choose to enroll them in religious education classes. Baylen learned a lot at these classes. "My teacher was really exciting, because she was always laughing, and we did interesting crafts and played fun games. The games helped me to learn and remember different stories from the Bible. We also learned a lot about the sacraments. My favorite sacrament is marriage, because I like the way two people make a promise to each other and say, 'I do.'"

Lia, another young student writer, also had the opportunity to attend religious education classes at her church, where children of all different ages go to "Children's Church." They leave Mass right after the first blessing, and return right before the Our Father prayer. While they are away, they play games, make crafts, and read and learn about their faith. Lia remembers learning a lot from a special book that had Bible stories, colorful illustrations, quizzes and art projects. Lia says, "Sometimes people think that since we only take religious education classes once a week, we don't learn very much, but we do! I think I have learned a lot about God at every single class."

Those children who are not attending religious education classes at their church may be enrolled in a Catholic school. Only some children have the opportunity to attend Catholic schools while they are growing up. James says, "I feel that I am lucky to have the chance to learn about my faith, and be a part of God's family even when I am at school. Sometimes it is not easy to be a Catholic, because other people don't understand my faith, or make fun of the things that I do. Being at a Catholic school helps because everyone there has the same beliefs, and we are able to share and learn with each other."

One of the easiest ways to identify a Catholic school is by its name. Most Catholic schools are named after a famous saint like Saint Louis or Saint Vincent de Paul. When you visit a Catholic school you will often find the children participating in a school Mass or learning about God and Jesus in religion class. Students study a lot about saints and listen to Bible stories. Sometimes a priest will come to the classrooms and teach different lessons about the

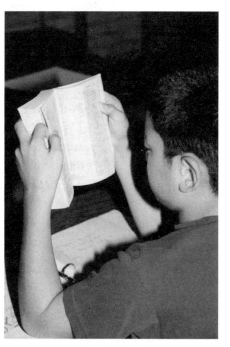

A young author checks his dictionary

faith. The Students like to ask Father questions.

For many, attending religion classes at church or a Catholic school are important parts of their Catholic experience. It is the beginning of their journey, and the first place where they see other children and adults living their faith. It is also the place where they learn about the seven important sacraments.

Throughout our lives as Catholics we may receive seven sacraments. A sacrament is a visible sign of God's grace in our lives. However, for Catholics the word sacrament means much more. It means that we are friends with God. With each sacrament, God gives himself to us and we move closer to God. We call Baptism, Confirmation, and Eucharist the three Sacraments of Initiation. Anointing of the Sick and Reconciliation are the two Sacraments of Healing. Holy Orders and Matrimony are the two Sacraments of Service. Sacraments are physical signs of God moving into our souls.

By receiving the sacraments, we are showing other people that we are in God's family. Before Jesus left us on earth, he gave us the seven sacraments to help us come closer to him, and guide us to heaven. The sacraments are one of the ways that God lives in our hearts and a means by which our souls become holy and beautiful. Grace is like a key that opens the door to heaven. Jesus loved us so much that he died on the cross so that we could go to heaven and have grace in our souls. Now we are going to tell you about each sacrament.

BAPTISM

Baylen Lessner

"My little brother, Mark, got really sick after he was born," one young author explained. "Liquid would build up in his back, and put a lot of strain on his neck and back. When he was seven days old, we took him to Children's Hospital. Mark had spinal meningitis. The doctors said he was not going to live. So we got Father Guida to baptize him. Father baptized him by putting holy water on Mark's forehead and hands. He couldn't be held because he was in intensive care. Father Guida put all his faith in God and so did my family. As soon as Mark was baptized, he started to get better. My life would have been a lot different if my brother had died. I thank God for not letting that happen."

Baptism usually takes place in a Catholic Church, and is done by a priest, but not always. In rare cases if people are sick or dying, they can get baptized in a hospital, and anyone can baptize in an emergency. To do this you have to take water, pour it on the person's head, and say, "I baptize you in the name of the Father,

A baby being baptized

and of the Son and of the Holy Spirit." If you don't have any water, you need to get some, but it does not have to be holy water.

Baptism is the first sacrament that Catholics receive. Without it Catholics can't receive any of the other sacraments. Baptism is the beginning of new life as we are cleansed from our original sin and welcomed into the Church for the first time.

People get baptized to enter into the family of God. Before your baptism, your mother and father picked out relatives or close friends to be your godparents.

Godparents help parents give the child a good education and training in the Catholic faith. Your parents pick one godmother and one godfather. As a gift at your baptism, you might receive a Bible or rosary from your parents or godparents. When a baby is baptized, the parents and godparents promise in the baby's name that he or she will learn about and practice the Catholic faith. When persons old enough to make promises themselves are baptized, the parents and godparents are there to witness and support the promises being made. These promises include keeping the Ten Commandments and following the rules of the Church.

When older people choose to be baptized into the Catholic religion, they will have to take classes called the Rite of Christian Initiation for Adults (RCIA). Kelly is in sixth grade and is not baptized yet, but she is going to become Catholic in this next year. When Kelly was little she saw other children receiving Holy Communion, and she would start to cry. She didn't know if Jesus was telling her something. Then she said to herself, "I am going to become Catholic." She thought there was a part of her missing. She also wants to receive this sacrament because she saw her father get baptized recently. Kelly has begun taking classes and will have the right to be confirmed with her Baptism next spring. From this story you can see that Baptism is very important to Kelly and God.

Jesus was baptized even though he had no sins. He wanted to set an example for all his people. The history behind baptism comes from the time of John the Baptist who was Jesus' cousin. John went around baptizing people and telling them about God. One day John was baptizing people and he told them that a man more powerful than him would come to baptize them not only with water but also with the Holy Spirit. Later, Jesus came to the Jordan River and asked for baptism from John. Jesus did this because he is both man and God. By asking for baptism from John, Jesus showed he is truly one with us. When Jesus was baptized he was saying yes to God to take away our sins. After this, Jesus told his apostles to go out and tell others about the Good News and baptize people in all nations.

Some churches have a special place called the baptistery, where the baptismal font is. During Baptism the priest pours water on your head or lowers you into a pool of water and lifts you out again while he says, "I baptize you in the name of the Father, and of the Son, and of the Holy Spirit." The holy water cleanses

candle, cloth, and holy water

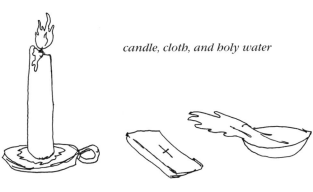

your heart and soul. Water reminds us of Jesus' baptism. Water is the instrument of grace. You also receive a white cloth and a white candle from the priest. The white candle is lit from the Easter Vigil candle and stands for faith. The white piece of cloth that is set over your shoulders is a sign of purity. The priest baptizes you in the name of the Father and of the Son and of the Holy Spirit. The priest traces a cross on your forehead, your mouth, and your hands. You are now part of the family of God.

RECONCILIATION

"My first confession was the most memorable moment in my life," a young author shared. "It made me feel revived, refreshed, and all out great. It started out embarrassing. When it is your first time, you might be afraid that the priest might laugh or yell at you, or that he will tell someone about your sins. However, when a man becomes a priest he promises to keep all confessions a secret. A priest cannot even answer questions about what people have told him in confession—even if a judge or policeman asks him! In the confessional, I was nervous. But once I got the hang of it, it was a cinch. Afterwards, I said my penance and felt completely new." The Pope says, "We must rediscover the full beauty of this sacrament....

Only those who have known the Father's tender embrace can pass on to others the same warmth."

Reconciliation, also known as confession, or the sacrament of Penance, is a sacrament of healing. In reconciliation God's peace is given to you and you are made new. Most baptized Catholics receive this sacrament around the age of seven or eight. It is a sacrament of God's grace and forgiveness. In this sacrament God frees us from sin and we receive his mercy and grace. We learn to be humble before God.

After you receive this sacrament for the first time you should go as often as possible. Reconciliation brings you closer to God. It makes you feel better about yourself and makes you better prepared to receive the Eucharist. Reconciliation is usually received in a church and can be celebrated by any priest. These leaders in the Church represent Jesus and can bring us God's forgiveness.

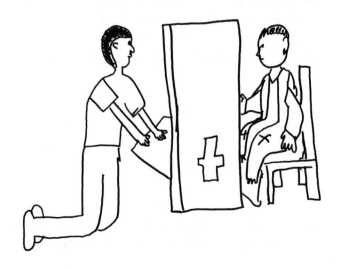

Live in God's light.
Proclaim the Gospel.
Do well.
Do it all over again.

Confession

There are several steps a person must take before and during the sacrament of Reconciliation. First, people examine their conscience by thinking about their own actions in relation to the Ten Commandments. They decide what mistakes they have made. Then, they need to feel sorry for hurting others and God and make a decision to try not to sin again. At this point a person is ready to confess (tell) their sins to a priest. They can sit down with a priest in a private room and talk to him face-to-face or they can go into a confessional (a small room divided by a screen) to speak to a priest. You begin by saying, "Forgive me, Father, for I have sinned. My last confession was…" and then you go ahead and tell your sins. After you tell him your sins, sometimes the priest will talk to you in a very nice way about how you can improve. Next, the priest will tell you to do a good deed, say some prayers, or read from the Bible. This is called penance. Afterwards, the priest will ask you to recite a special Catholic prayer called the Act of Contrition and then the priest will give you a blessing called an absolution to free you from your sins. Finally, you thank the priest, do your penance and try to live a better life.

As people are thinking about what they have done wrong for confession, they must consider the two different kinds of sin, a venial sin and a mortal sin. To commit a mortal sin, something must be a serious sin and you must know that it is serious and deliberately do it anyway. A mortal sin completely breaks a person's ties with God. A venial sin is less serious and only weakens one's relationship with God. To find out what a sin is, look at the Ten Commandments, which are laws that were given to Moses from God. The Commandments help us to stay close to God and if they have been broken then we have sinned. Here is a list of the Com-

Student author at work on this chapter

Honor your mother and father

mandments and suggestions for how to follow them.

1 I am the Lord your God. You shall not have other gods besides me—We worship only one God. We worship the Most Holy Trinity: God the Father, God the Son, and God the Holy Spirit. We can't see anything as more important than God.

2 You shall not take the name of the Lord, your God, in vain—We should only use God's name in prayer and in holiness. God's name is powerful and we should respect that.

3 Remember to keep holy the Lord's Day—Participating at Mass on Sunday or Saturday evening is important because it helps us keep close to God. God wants to talk to us and hear from us. We should also spend time with our families in church and at home on Sundays because God wants us to rest and enjoy this special day.

4 Honor your father and mother—We need to obey and respect our parents, teachers, and others in charge of us.

5 You shall not kill—We must not take the life of anyone else or our own lives. Also, we must not hurt the feelings of others or hit or kick other people.

6 You shall not commit adultery—If you have a wife or husband you should not want anyone else. God is with you, as you love your husband or wife. We need to respect the bodies of others and not lead them into sin.

7 You shall not steal—Stealing offends God and the person someone steals from. We must not take anything that does not belong to us.

8 You shall not bear false witness against your neighbor—We must not lie. We should not say untrue things about our neighbor. We should also speak up when we know the truth.

9 You shall not covet your neighbor's wife—Coveting is a word that means wanting something else really bad. You are so jealous that you want something with an evil desire. You should not want someone else's wife. If you have a wife you should love her with all your heart. Men and women are not possessions.

10 You shall not covet your neighbor's belongings—We shouldn't want or be jealous of other people's things.

S is for sorrow for our sins.
I is for inside we know our sins are wrong.
N is for never, never turn away from God!!

Saint Charles Borromeo started the private confessional with a chair and screens around it. Today we may also go to a community Penance service that starts with prayers and songs and then continues with each person going to a priest and making a private confession.

It is good to receive the sacrament of Reconciliation as often as possible. Most Catholic churches offer times for confession on Saturday, by appointment, or at communal services during Advent and Lent. During the year you can go as many times as you want. By receiving this sacrament, we are forgiven by God, given special graces and return to the community to live a better life.

HOLY EUCHARIST

For fourteen years Chester played the guitar at Catholic Masses, even though he was not Catholic. He watched many people in their suits and dresses receive the Eucharist. He knew that something was missing in his life. His friends told him he could receive the Eucharist because he believed in Christ, but in his heart he knew it was wrong. Watching all the people going to Communion inspired Chester to become a Catholic. This past year he was baptized. He was so inspired he wrote a song about the mysteries of our faith.

The Holy Eucharist is one of the Sacraments of Initiation and is usually the third sacrament that Catholics receive. The word "Eucharist" means thanksgiving in Greek. This is one of the most special sacraments in our faith because in it we take Jesus into our own bodies. The sacrament of Holy Eucharist is a special celebration at church, where we all share a meal together.

First Communion Day

Luke remembers receiving his First Holy Communion. "When I was in second grade, I received the Holy Eucharist. It was a special ceremony at church and I was there with all my classmates. We got dressed up and felt proud because we were receiving Jesus into our bodies for the first time. Afterwards, we knew that we would always carry Jesus in our hearts. Our family and friends celebrated with us. It was a wonderful day."

This sacrament goes back to the time of Jesus and his apostles. Before Jesus was about to die on the cross, he shared a meal with his apostles. We call this meal, the Last Supper. Jesus blessed bread and wine and turned them into his Body and Blood. Jesus then shared this meal with his friends and asked them to always do this in his memory. This was the beginning of this special sacrament.

People who are Catholic still can share this meal of Jesus' Body and Blood every time they go to Mass. Before receiving this sacrament, you must be baptized, showing that you are part of God's family, and have a clean soul and be free from serious sin. If an important guest was coming to our house, we would want to make certain it was clean. It is great to do the same thing before we receive Jesus. If you have a serious sin, you should go to confession before receiving Communion. Also, for at least one hour before Communion you should not eat, chew gum or drink anything except water, so your body is prepared to receive Jesus.

Sunday Mass is not the only time or place that you can receive the Body and Blood of Jesus. Some people receive the Eucharist more often and go to Mass every day. There are also many places where you can receive the Eucharist, such as, homes, chapels, hospitals, or even outdoors. Sometimes a priest, deacon, or Eucharistic minister will put a consecrated

Host in a special container called a pyx, and deliver it to those who are too old or sick to go Mass.

There are two different ways to receive the Eucharist. The first way is to make an altar or throne with your hands by putting one on top of the other. The priest holds up the Host in front of you and says, "The Body of Christ" and you must respond by saying, "Amen." When you say "Amen," you are saying yes to God and telling people that you believe in Jesus. Then you put the Host in your mouth and swallow it. If you are going to receive the Precious Blood, you must also

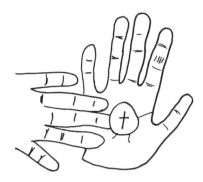

say "Amen" before taking a drink. The second way to receive the Eucharist is by having the priest or minister place the Host directly on your tongue and swallowing it.

Catholics all around the world take special pride in this sacrament. They believe that by taking Jesus' Body and Blood into their body they are coming closer to God and making him happy. They carry Jesus in their hearts every day and try to spread his message to others.

A cake to celebrate the great day

Checking over this chapter

CONFIRMATION

"I have been a Catholic since I was little. In April of 1999 I received the sacrament of Confirmation. It was a great feeling to be sealed with the Holy Spirit. I felt very happy after being confirmed because I really learned a lot about my faith during my Confirmation classes. Now that I am confirmed, I try to make sure that I live my faith more fully by attending Mass regularly and going to confession. Because I understand these sacraments better, they mean more to me and now I can be a good example to others."

Mr. Dan, a high school student who worked on this book, shared the above statements about the sacrament of Confirmation. He and all his classmates were confirmed by a bishop. Dan chose his older sister, Sarah, to be his sponsor, because he knew that she would help him to grow and understand his own faith.

During Dan's Confirmation classes he learned that it is important to help others. He completed the community service hours that he needed before he could be confirmed. At first, Dan was not excited about spending his free time helping others, but then he realized that it was very rewarding and a lot of fun.

Mr. Matt, another high school student who helped with this book, remembers a

A young man being confirmed

Leike

very important piece of advice that the archbishop told him and his classmates. "After confirming us in the Holy Spirit, the archbishop said, 'Go out and look forward to the things in front of you.'" Mr. Matt looks forward to putting his faith into action through serving others and defending his faith.

The first Confirmation happened on Pentecost, which was an event that happened after Jesus' ascension into heaven, when the apostles needed help. The apostles were filled with the Holy Spirit, when tongues of fire appeared above their heads, and they heard a strong wind. Afterwards, the apostles had new courage and strength and began to speak about everything Jesus had taught them. This first Confirmation has given us the traditional symbols for the Holy Spirit, which include the dove, the light of candles or fire, and the wind.

Today, people receiving the sacrament of Confirmation must have already received the sacraments of Baptism, Penance and Eucharist. In the United States our bishops have said that the usual time to receive Confirmation is between the ages of seven to sixteen. People who join the Rite of Christian Initiation for Adults (RCIA) may also receive it at an older age.

Daniel, a student writer shared this experience with our group. He was confirmed at the age of nine, during the

same ceremony at which his father received this sacrament. It was a very special event for Daniel's entire family because Daniel's mother served as their sponsor. Daniel remembers going to special classes with his dad for six months. He read from the Bible and learned so much about his faith. "My favorite parts were the projects we did," said Daniel. "One time we got to participate in the food box and I collected money to help poor people buy food." Daniel and his father were both confirmed at the Easter Vigil, the Mass on the Saturday night before Easter Sunday. Although Daniel was

Gifts Of The Holy Spirit

helps us become wiser. *Understanding* helps us listen to others. *Right judgment* helps us make the right choice. *Courage* helps us be brave in hard times. *Knowledge* helps us use what we know and teach others. *Reverence* helps us show respect for God. *Fear of the Lord,* the last gift, helps us realize the wonder and awe of God.

The sacrament of Confirmation is usually celebrated in the spring at a special Mass in the church. Your friends and family, members of the parish, and your sponsor will help celebrate and witness this special time in your young Catholic life. During the Mass, the candidates and their sponsors are called to the front of the church and asked to make the same promises that their parents made for them at baptism. The sponsors and the rest of the community then join them in prayer. The candidates are anointed with holy oil called chrism. The oil represents a spiritual seal, a sign of abundance and joy, cleanliness and strength, healing, beauty, and health. An archbishop or bishop usually performs this sacrament and lays his hands on each candidate to seal them with the Holy Spirit.

Confirmation is the third Sacrament of Initiation. It is usually received as the fourth sacrament in the journey of faith. It gives us the grace of the Holy Spirit and is the first time that a person accepts the responsibilities of the Catholic faith. Confirmation is a sign that a person has become an adult member of the Catholic faith.

a little nervous before the ceremony began, he was also very excited because he and his dad were going to be filled with the grace and power of the Holy Spirit.

Most candidates will take a special confirmation name, usually the name of a saint, as someone they believe will continue to help them live out their faith. Chaylyn, a high school mentor, chose Saint Theresa because she had learned a lot about this saint from a guest speaker and she likes roses, which are the symbol for Saint Theresa.

Young Catholics also learn about the seven gifts of the Holy Spirit during their Confirmation classes. These gifts include wisdom, understanding, right judgment, courage, knowledge, reverence, and fear of the Lord. Each of these gifts helps us to live out our faith in a better way. *Wisdom*

MATRIMONY

As Cathleen walked down the aisle, she felt nervous because she was about to get married. She had taken all the marriage classes, been to the dress rehearsal and knew she was ready because she had frequently received Communion and the sacrament of Reconciliation. She had also been praying for a good marriage. Then she remembered the wonderful things God had promised her, and this helped her to relax.

The name of the sacrament by which a baptized man and a baptized woman join together for life in marriage is Matrimony. Matrimony is a sacrament of service. It was created when God made Adam and Eve. First, he made man who was bored and lonely, so then he made woman. They were told to love each other and to have children. The love and commitment between a married couple shows the love and commitment between Christ and his Church. It is a tough choice because being married is like being chained to someone for the rest of your life. So, it is important to know the person very well. You can do this by treating each other nicely and not leading each other into sin. If someone is not prepared for such a special commitment, they should not go through with it because it might offend God.

During most Catholic marriages, the bride and groom recite vows in front of Jesus, their family and friends. The vows are promises to be faithful to each other and never break their bond of love. They also promise to be open to having children, who are gifts from God. These promises make the marriage complete. The bride and groom are then blessed and are joined together as one Body in Christ. The priest does this at the church, which is God's house. The man and woman give rings to each other because the ring is a symbol of their never-ending love and of the couple's hope that their marriage will last forever. Once the rings are blessed, they're worn on the third finger of the left hand to show that the two people are married.

Photo credit: Danielson family

A wedding ceremony

A traditional wedding includes a bride, a groom, bridesmaids and groomsmen, who are friends and family of the bride and the groom. Sometimes children are also in the wedding, like a ring bearer who carries the rings and a little flower girl who throws petals down before the bride walks down the aisle. Everyone in the wedding dresses up. Once the ceremony is over, people sometimes blow bubbles or throw rice as the bride and groom walk through the crowd. Then the people line up and the couple says hello to everyone.

The Bible says that people should not get divorced. Jesus doesn't like divorce. He says, "That which God has united must not be divided." Sometimes this is difficult because of problems, but making sacrifices and working together are important parts of this special commitment. Everyone should remember that marriage is a very special sacrament, which reminds us of Jesus' love for the Church. And so it should be treated with care, respect and commitment to last a lifetime.

All married people have a responsibility to keep their vows and to always love each other. They do this by keeping their marriage holy. For example, some couples may pray the rosary, read the Bible, or put their faith into action by teaching a religious education class together. It's good for them to pray together because this helps a couple stay together.

A happy wedding party

Photo credit: Rox's Images

HOLY ORDERS

When you look at a priest, can you imagine the hundreds of people he will baptize? Do you think of the thousands of people he will forgive in the sacrament of Reconciliation, or the million people he will give Holy Communion to? A priest helps thousands and thousands of people to be holy. Is there any other vocation where you could help so many people?

The tradition of our Catholic Church teaches us that Holy Orders is a Sacrament of Service that only men can receive. (Jesus' twelve apostles were men.) It makes these men more like Jesus. It gives them the power to serve the people of God.

The Last Supper was the first time Jesus showed his apostles how to consecrate bread and wine making them his Body and Blood. Jesus also gave them the power to forgive sins, baptize, confirm, and later join a couple in marriage.

Today, men receive Holy Orders after they study for many years. First, they must have a college degree, usually in philosophy, which is the study of basic questions about life. Then some men have a year of spirituality where they pray and reflect. Lastly, they study theology, which is the study of religion, for four years. Men who have received all of the other sacraments, except Matrimony and the Anointing of the Sick, are at least twenty-three years old, have been a deacon, and have studied how to be a priest, can then receive the sacrament of Holy Orders.

In a cathedral, during a Mass with music and prayer, the men who are being ordained are called up to the altar by a bishop, archbishop, cardinal, or Pope and asked if they are ready to become priests. Their teachers and all the people present are also asked if these men are ready to become priests. The young men are asked if they "promise to be faithful and obedient to God, the bishop and his successors, for the rest of their lives." Next, the men

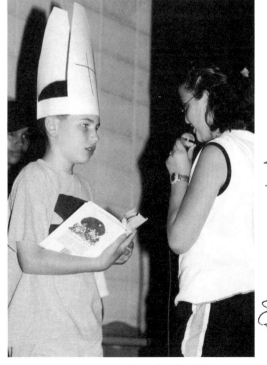

Learning about the role of a bishop

lie on their stomachs, with their arms above their heads like Superman. We think this is because they are laying down their lives for Jesus. They are praying real hard about giving their lives to the Lord.

At the same time, the people at the ceremony usually sing the names of many great saints and ask them to pray for all the men who are becoming priests. This is called the Litany of the Saints. It is a way to call blessings down from the saints for the priests. After this, the bishop will lay his hands upon the men's heads. The new priests will then kneel and the other priests in attendance will lay their hands on the heads of the newly ordained and offer silent prayers. Then the long prayer of consecration (dedication) is said by the bishop. This prayer makes them members of the priesthood of Jesus Christ. However, the ceremony continues, as another priest will help place a chasuble, or priest's robe, on the newly ordained men. Toward the end of the ceremony, the men will have their hands blessed with a special oil called chrism. This allows them to be able to consecrate the bread and the wine and make it the Body and Blood of Christ.

Some priests remember their bodies tingling during the ceremony. We think this is the power of the Holy Spirit and because they feel happy and they are now closer to God. At the end of the ceremony, the men go through a line giving each other the Kiss of Peace.

After the ordination, the new priest's family usually gives him a reception. It is a great celebration, almost like a wedding reception. As a priest, this man can now proclaim the Gospel, celebrate

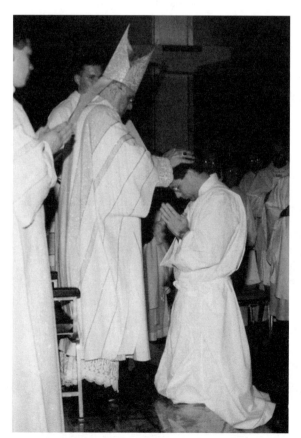

A young man being ordained a priest

Mass, preach to all the people, and administer six of the seven sacraments. Only a bishop can administer the sacrament of Holy Orders and, like Baptism and Confirmation, this is a sacrament received just once.

The sacrament of Holy Orders has three levels. The first or top level is bishops. It is only bishops who have the power to ordain other priests and to pass on the apostles' mission. The second level is priests. Priests can say Mass and serve the Church, but they don't have as much power as a bishop. The third level is deacons. Deacons do not hear confessions, celebrate Mass or anoint, but they are able to marry people, baptize, bury and help the priest to spread the Word of God during Mass. Deacons can be married.

Holy Orders is important because it is the sacrament that allows men to serve God by making Jesus sacramentally present in them. Those who have received Holy Orders preach and teach the Good News, they help us serve those in need, they lead God's people in celebrating the sacraments, and they help build a Christian community. To be a bishop, priest, or deacon you should be kind and loving, trust God, and have a great deal of patience.

ANOINTING OF THE SICK

Tons of people crowded around Jesus and bumped into him. They all wanted to meet him. A woman wanted to touch his clothing because she had been sick for twelve years. She kept saying, "I need to touch Jesus to get better!" Then she shoved and pushed her way through the crowd until finally she touched him! All of a sudden she felt better. Jesus stopped and he said, "Who touched me?" "Anyone could have touched you," answered the apostles. "But I felt power going out of me," Jesus said. Then the woman said, "I did." And Jesus said, "You are better now because of your faith."

One day a religious man was driving his car when suddenly there were sounds of screeching tires, honking horns, and sudden gasps. Then there was silence. The driver was dead. After receiving the news, the man's family was in shock. They could not believe that their father, who had gone to church regularly for years, had died without having been anointed. The man's family was very sad. However, one night their phone rang and it was a Catholic priest. He told the family he had been on his way to a picnic when he saw their father's terrible accident. The priest had given their father the blessings of the Anointing of the Sick, before his death. The family knew the priest had been sent to the accident by God. They believed that their father had been truly devoted to God and God had cared for them in their time of sadness.

A diligent author at work

In the two stories above we see a woman healed and we hear about a man who was given a blessing at death. Blessings and healing are both a part of the sacrament called Anointing of the Sick. It is a sacrament which brings peace and comfort to a sick or dying person and his or her family.

In the sacrament of the Anointing of the Sick, God does the healing and we do the praying. There are many stories of Jesus and the apostles healing people. One of the most widely known includes Jesus healing the man with leprosy (a skin disease that leaves many sores on the body). One day Jesus was just walking along when a poor man who had leprosy came up to him. He said, "Lord, if you wish, you can make me healthy." Stretching out his hand, Jesus touched him and said, "I will heal you." Right after he said this the man was completely healed. Jesus then told him not to tell anybody, but to show himself to the priest. Jesus then said, "Offer your healing to God" (Mk 1:40–45).

Another popular story of healing was when a crippled man was healed by Jesus' apostles Peter and John. As the apostles were walking to the temple (a place of worship for Jews), for the three o'clock service, they passed a crippled man begging for food. The man had been crippled since birth. Peter and John stopped in front of the man and Peter said, "In the name of Jesus the Nazarean, rise up and walk." The man jumped up and walked with Peter and John into the

temple. When people saw this they were amazed (Acts 3:1–9).

In the early days of the Church, oil was used to heal people and the sacrament was called Extreme Unction or the Last Rites. It was only for the dying. The dying person also received Communion and the sacrament of Reconciliation. He or she was anointed on the eyelids, feet, hands, mouth, nose and ears. The sign of the cross was made on each part of the body. After Vatican II, a meeting with the Pope and the bishops of the Church, this sacrament received a better name. It is now called the Anointing of the Sick. Today this sacrament can be received by sick people, too, and can be celebrated at Mass, at home, or at the hospital. It helps people who are suffering and prepares them for heaven.

A person can receive the Anointing of the Sick as often as needed. Many Catholic churches offer this sacrament once a month. As part of a special Healing Mass, the priest anoints the people's hands and foreheads with oil by making a cross and saying, "Through this holy anointing, may the Lord in his love and mercy help you with the grace of the Holy Spirit. May the Lord who frees you from sin save you and raise you up. Amen."

GOING HOME TO GOD

We have spent most of this chapter talking about growing up Catholic. But we have not talked about what it's like to die as a Catholic. A lot of people think this is a sad or scary time, but if a person has lived their Catholic faith, it isn't. We know that our loved one or friend has gone ahead to be with the Lord. We'll learn about growing up and dying Catholic with the help of one of our writer's grandmothers.

Martha's First Communion

Richard Deanda's grandmother was born August 1, 1940, and given the name Martha Virginia Herrera. Martha lived her whole life in Denver, Colorado. She was baptized, September 15, 1940, at Holy Ghost Church. She received the sacrament of Reconciliation for the first time in July of 1948. After that Martha made her First Communion at Saint Cajetan's Church. A little later in her life, on April 2, 1950, Martha received Confirmation.

When she was in her twenties, Martha Herrera married Richard Thomas Deanda. That was on April

Martha's wedding day

29, 1961, at Saint Joseph's Church. Their children received all of their sacraments at Saint Joseph's Church, and Mrs. Deanda worked as the church secretary.

Mrs. Deanda often told her children that they could always talk to God and bring their problems to him just like she did. She had a great devotion to our Blessed Mother. Everyone remembers her praying the rosary every day. In her free time, she made rosaries and gave them to different people. She loved making all kinds of things and always baked and decorated cakes for every birthday or special occasion in her children and grandchildren's lives.

One very special event in Mrs. Deanda's life happened on April 14, 1979. She and her family went on a pilgrimage to Rome and guess what? They were there when Pope John Paul II celebrated his first Easter Vigil as Pope. Not many people can say they saw that.

Mrs. Deanda suffered for many years with rheumatoid arthritis but never stopped praying her rosary and living her faith. After a while she knew it was time to get ready to meet the Lord. She started preparing and doing little things, like leaving out family recipes where people could find them. When she went to the hospital on May 29, 2001, she asked her family to call the priest. Father gave her the Anointing of the Sick and she went to confession and received Communion on May 31, 2001. Shortly after that, she went into a coma. She was at peace and ready to go home to God.

During our writing workshop, Richard made a rosary for his grandma. He took it to her and gave it to her right before she died. He was there with his family praying for his grandma as she passed away on June 18, 2001. Martha Virginia Deanda had a beautiful funeral Mass, three days later, on Richard's eleventh birthday. She was buried holding the rosary Richard gave her.

All through Martha Virginia Deanda's journey, her Catholic faith was a beautiful part of her life. It helped her live life well and die knowing she was near the end of her journey to meet the Lord.

As you can see, the sacraments are a very important part of our Catholic faith. Through the blessings received at each one, you can fill your soul and heart with grace. The initiation sacraments of Baptism, Holy Eucharist, and Confirmation help you enter into the family of God. The sacraments of service, Holy Orders and Matrimony, are the ways we serve God by serving others. The healing sacraments of Reconciliation and Anointing of the Sick cleanse your soul, bringing you graces from God.

Being Catholic is a big part of who we are as people. We learn about God from the Church, our parents, godparents, and teachers. God the Father, the Son and the Holy Spirit are there for us every step of the way. Growing up Catholic is an exciting way to go!

Martha Deanda's funeral

PRAISE AND CELEBRATION

A Look at the Mass and Catholic Worship

Mass is a celebration,
Oh, it's quite a sensation.
We praise the Lord and his holy name.
Nothing else is quite the same.

Catholics have many different ways to worship and talk to God. The most important is the Mass. We also have special services and blessed objects that help us pray. This chapter starts by explaining the Mass. Then it covers the Church year and different ways to pray. It ends by describing different kinds of prayer.

Singing practice before Mass

THE MASS

The Mass, or Eucharistic Celebration, is heaven and earth together. It is being gathered by God and is a great celebration of love. It is a wonderful blessing when everyone can share Jesus' Body and Blood. We know that Jesus is really present with us, especially in the Eucharist. The Mass is a story of love that unfolds every week.

The first Mass was the Last Supper, where Jesus shared the meal with his twelve apostles on the night before he died. Jesus prayed over the bread and wine and told the apostles to do this in memory of him.

Now Mass is celebrated every day all over the world. Our Sunday Mass is a special celebration in honor of Jesus' resurrection. Jesus asked us to do this in memory of him.

When we go to church on Saturday evening or Sunday and see a friend, we wave at each other. We gather together in

The gathering song

Mass reminds us of a family reunion, because everyone is there and the church looks nice. There is an altar with candles, which reminds us of a party. Everyone who comes to this special celebration comes to be with God. Whether happy or sad, they come to be with God.

The Mass is divided into two parts. We call these parts the Liturgy of the Word and the Liturgy of the Eucharist.

At the beginning of Mass, the priest says "Hello" by leading us in prayer. Next, we tell God we are sorry for not always loving him and other people. Then we say the echo prayer, "Lord have mercy, Christ have mercy, Lord have mercy." After our prayer of sorrow, we sometimes offer a prayer of praise that sounds like the angels at Christmas. "Glory to God in the highest and peace to his people on earth."

the church, and all kinds of people smile at us. Some people we know, and others we have never met. However, we all belong to the same family.

Most churches have someone at the door to greet people. This helps us feel welcomed and not rushed. After we enter church, we sing the gathering song. This helps us think about God.

Did you know that some people think that Catholics don't sing? But we do! Singing is a great way to praise the Lord. When we sing, we feel free, just like a bird. When we sing in church, we are worshiping God. It is God's house, and he loves to hear us praise him. It's great to think that God sings along with us when we are in church.

A young author proclaims God's Word in the First Reading

Next, we listen to words from the Bible. The First Reading is usually taken from the Old Testament. One favorite story is the story of Moses. This is the Old Testament story that is told every year at the Easter Vigil Mass.

One day when Moses was out chasing a lamb, he found a burning bush. God spoke to Moses through the bush. God told Moses to tell the Pharaoh to let his people go. So Moses went to Pharaoh, and asked him if the Israelites could leave. Pharaoh refused. Moses went back to Pharaoh again, and again Pharaoh refused. Pharaoh still refused even when the plagues of frogs and locusts came upon the Egyptian people. Only after the tenth plague, when the Angel of Death killed the first born son in every Egyptian home did Pharaoh say, "Okay. Go!"

Moses led the Israelites to the Red Sea. Suddenly, Pharaoh and his army came racing over the hill toward the Israelites. That's when Moses parted the sea with God's help, and the Israelites got away. The Old Testament always points us to the New Testament.

After the Old Testament reading, we have the Responsorial Psalm. We can sing or say the words. Responsorial psalms thank and praise God. David wrote many of the psalms.

A favorite psalm is Psalm 97. It is about singing a new song to God because he is good and has created beautiful things.

Following the Responsorial Psalm, we read from the New Testament. These stories are about the disciples and the early Christians. Next we stand and sing "Alleluia." We are praising God, and getting ready to listen to the Gospel lesson. Standing shows how really important Jesus' words are!

The Gospel readings tell stories about Jesus' life from the books of Matthew, Mark, Luke and John. Some of the Gospels are parables, and easier to understand. Other Gospels are stories from the life of Jesus, like the time Jesus decided to be baptized by his cousin, John the Baptist.

"You should be baptizing me," said John, when Jesus got there.

"I want YOU to baptize me," Jesus said.

"Okay," John replied.

John put Jesus' face into the water. As Jesus got up, a white dove flew through the air. This was a symbol of the Holy Spirit.

The Gospel is followed by the homily. That's when the priest or deacon explains the readings and makes them easier to understand, and helps us see how they touch our lives.

Following the homily, we say the Creed together. We tell God and each other that we believe what God told us. We believe in the Father, in Jesus Christ, in the Holy Spirit, and in the holy Catholic Church.

Then we say the petitions. We ask for special help. We also ask God to help the people in the world.

Next comes the Preparation of the Gifts. To show that we love God and each other, we give money for the Church and the poor. Then people in the church take

Preparing to make the collection for the Church and the poor

turns bringing the bread and wine to the altar. The priest blesses the bread and wine in preparation for the Consecration. This is a time in the Mass when we often sing a song about offering ourselves to God.

Then we sing or say together, "Holy, Holy, Holy Lord," because we are coming to the most sacred time in the Mass. Then the priest consecrates the bread and wine by saying the same words that Jesus said at the Last Supper.

Jesus took bread and said, "This is my Body, which will be given up for you. Do this in memory of me." Then he took the cup and said, "This is my Blood, the Blood of the new and everlasting covenant. It will be shed for you and for all so that sins may be forgiven. Do this in memory of me."

The consecration: the bread becomes the Body of Christ

After the priest consecrates the bread and wine they are the Body and Blood of Jesus Christ even though they still look and taste like bread and wine.

Next, we say aloud the main mystery of our faith: "Christ has died. Christ is risen. Christ will come again." This is what we believe.

Then we say the prayer that Jesus himself taught us, the "Our Father." All Christians have this prayer.

Now we're ready to shake hands with our neighbors as we offer each other the Sign of Peace. This gets us set to share Communion together as a family.

Following the Sign of Peace, we say or sing another echo prayer. "Lamb of God, you take away the sins of the world, have mercy on us." We say this three times.

Then we end with the thought "Grant us peace."

Communion is awesome! It is the most important thing we do. We believe Communion says, "I love you, Lord." The bread is Jesus' Body! The wine is Jesus' Blood! Anyone who eats his Body and drinks his Blood will live forever. This is what we believe.

To prepare for Communion, we have already fasted for an hour. We must also be free of serious sin. Just before Communion, we say together, "O Lord I am not worthy to receive you, but only say the word and I shall be healed."

If we are baptized Catholics and prepared to receive Jesus, we can join the procession to receive Holy Communion. If someone joins the procession and is not prepared to receive Communion, they should cross their arms across their chest. They will receive a blessing from the priest or the Eucharistic minister.

Often there is a song during Communion time that helps us think and pray about this great miracle called the Eucha-

rist. Since the word "Eucharist" means thanksgiving, this is the time when we are especially grateful to God. When we receive Jesus we thank him for coming to us. We speak to him about everything that is in our heart.

At the end of Mass, the priest says to everyone, "The Mass is ended. Go in peace to love and serve the Lord." And we answer all together, "Thanks be to God."

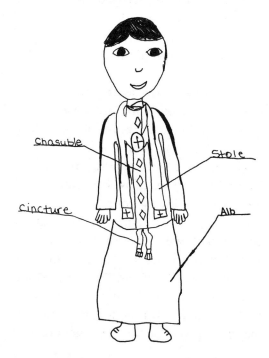

THE LITURGICAL YEAR

Jesus is with us all the time.
He speaks to us quietly in our minds.
We know that he is always there.
We think we are the perfect pair.
Jesus calls us his best friends.
We know our friendship will
never end.

The liturgical year is the Church celebrating the events of Christ's life and the feast days of Mary and the saints. The liturgical seasons are Advent, Christmastime, Lent, Eastertime and Ordinary Time, which comes between the great seasons.

The season of Advent begins four weeks before Christmas. This time helps us prepare for Christmas.

Christmas is the day when Jesus was born. This is one of the most joyful of all holidays throughout the world, when many people give gifts and toys to each other. Epiphany is the celebration when the three wise men traveled all the way to Bethlehem just to see Jesus. They gave him gifts of gold, myrrh, and frankincense.

Lent is a time that helps us get ready for Easter. It begins on Ash Wednesday and ends forty days later. The last week of Lent is called Holy Week. During Lent we try to pay more attention to doing good deeds, praying and making some sacrifices. Many Catholics give up something like watching television. Other people might say a special prayer or go to Mass more often. Also, during Lent, Catholics do not eat meat on Fridays. This has been a tradition since the first century to remember Jesus on the day that he died.

The Triduum is made up of the three holiest days of the year at the end of Holy Week. These days are: Holy Thursday, Good Friday, and Holy Saturday.

The word "triduum" looks hard to say, but it's simple. "Tri" has a short "i" as in "trip." "Du" sounds the same as in "do something." And "um" is just like saying "um." Put it together and you get Triduum, or three days.

Holy Thursday is the celebration of the Last Supper, when Jesus offered the bread and wine to God so it would become his Body and Blood. Our Catholic Church has a special ceremony to celebrate Holy Thursday. It in-

cludes the washing of the feet, like Jesus did for his apostles, to show his love.

Good Friday is the day when Jesus went through a whole lot of pain and suffering. He died for our sins because he loves us. Good Friday is the only day of the year when we don't have Mass. But we do have a Celebration of the Lord's Passion. It is made up of three parts. The first part is the Liturgy of the Word, when we listen to readings from the Bible. The second part is the Veneration of the Cross. That is when we touch or kiss the cross and think about Jesus. The third part is the Service of Communion. Even though the priest doesn't consecrate the bread and wine on Good Friday, he takes Hosts from the tabernacle that were already consecrated on

Holy Thursday. And so on Good Friday we can also receive Holy Communion.

Holy Saturday is the day after Jesus died on the cross and was put in the tomb. This is the evening of the Easter Vigil, our holiest night of the Church year.

Easter Vigil at the Cathedral of the Immaculate Conception smells like wonderful incense! The church starts out all dark, with no lights at all. They light a fire in a big pot that has wood in it. (At some churches where there is space, they make a bonfire outside instead of inside the church.) The people gather around the fire. The priest prays and lights the Easter or Paschal candle from the fire. Then he sings "Christ, our light." All the people sing back, "Thanks be to God."

Next the people follow the priest to the door of the church while he carries the lit candle. He sings again, "Christ, our light." And the people answer, "Thanks be to

God." All the people are holding small candles. Now the priest lights some of the people's candles from the big Paschal candle. Then these people light their neighbor's and pass the light on. Soon the whole church is lit with candles. Even with only this candlelight, we think the church is brighter than at any other time of the year!

Now everyone follows the priest right down the center aisle. Then he sings for the third time, "Christ, our light." And the people sing, "Thanks be to God."

In the Liturgy of the Word we hear special readings from the Bible. We always hear about Moses leading the Israelites out of Egypt. Sometimes we hear about the creation, Adam and Eve, Abraham and Isaac, and other Old Testament people. It's long, but it brings us closer to God. Readings from the New Testament and Gospel come next. All these readings seem to go on forever, just like God's love!

After the readings and the priest's homily, baptisms and confirmations are celebrated. People of any age can receive the sacraments they haven't received yet. This is also when people who want to become Catholics can join the Church if they've studied for it. This year, at the cathedral,

our new bishop, Bishop Gomez, did the baptisms. Archbishop Chaput welcomed the *confirmandi* (the people who want to be confirmed) and anointed them by putting special oil on their foreheads.

After the sacraments, we continue to celebrate Mass like we do every Sunday. At Communion time, the new Catholics get to receive their First Holy Communion. Easter Vigil Mass is the longest Mass of the year, but it is also the biggest celebration. At the end, we feel really blessed and holy.

Now we are officially at the Easter season of the liturgical year! This is the most glorious time of the year, when we rejoice at Jesus' love for us and our salvation. This season lasts for fifty days, through Ascension Day, until Pentecost.

On Pentecost, we celebrate the birthday of the Church. The dove, wind and tongues of fire symbolize Pentecost. That is when the Holy Spirit came down on the apostles and blessed them so they could speak in different languages and spread the Good News about Jesus everywhere.

The seasons following Christmastime and Eastertime are called Ordinary Time. But they are not so ordinary!

For instance, in February there are two special feasts. On February 2nd, there is Candlemas Day, when candles for the entire year are blessed. The next day, February 3rd, we celebrate the feast of Saint Blase, who was a bishop. On that day, the priest uses the new candles from the day before to bless our throats. This is because Bishop Blase is the patron saint of being healed of diseases of the throat. One time Bishop Blase was on a trip and a boy was choking on a fishbone. Bishop Blase criss-crossed two candles upon the boy's throat and prayed, and the boy was healed.

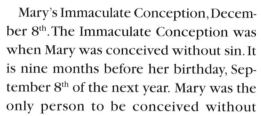

Then in March there is Saint Patrick's feast on the 17th, and Saint Joseph's Day on the 19th. We celebrate the feast of Saints Peter and Paul on June 29th. In fact, we celebrate saints' feasts all year long, but especially on November 1st, All Saints' Day, which is also a holy day of obligation.

Holy days of obligation are the days besides Sundays that faithful Catholics should go to Mass. Holy days are celebrated according to the needs of the people and the decisions of the bishops in each country. Sometimes the bishop or archbishop moves the celebration of a holy day to the next Sunday. Here is the list of six holy days that Catholics in United States celebrate:

Mary's Immaculate Conception, December 8th. The Immaculate Conception was when Mary was conceived without sin. It is nine months before her birthday, September 8th of the next year. Mary was the only person to be conceived without original sin, so she could be the Mother of God.

The Birth of Christ, December 25th. The birth of Christ is most commonly known as Christmas. This holy day is celebrated all around the world by attending Mass. It is also known as the Nativity. Many churches and houses have the nativity scene with the Magi, farm animals and shepherds. Most importantly, the Holy Family is in the stable. Some families wait until midnight on Christmas Eve to put the baby Jesus in the manger.

The Solemnity of Mary, Mother of God, January 1st (except when it falls on a Saturday or Monday). This is the day when we honor Mary as the Mother of God. This day is also eight days after the Birth of Jesus, and the day when Jesus was circumcised. Circumcision is the Jewish custom of consecrating the boys to God.

The Ascension of our Lord Jesus, 40 days after Easter (or in some western dioceses, the following Sunday). On Ascension Day Jesus returned to God in heaven and left the earth. Right before he left the apostles, he promised to send the Holy Spirit to guide them. The Holy Spirit did come on Pentecost ten days later, proving that Jesus always keeps his word.

The Assumption of the Blessed Virgin Mary, August 15th (except when it falls on a Saturday or Monday). This day celebrates the day the Blessed Virgin Mary was assumed into heaven, body and soul, to sit on the throne next to Jesus.

All Saints' Day, November 1st (except when it falls on a Saturday or Monday). On All Saints' Day we honor all of the saints. All Saints' Day is the day after Halloween (October 31st), and is a much more important day, even if it is less celebrated.

Catholics in Canada celebrate two holy days: the Solemnity of Mary, the Mother of God on January 1st and Christmas on December 25th.

The Church Setting

We believe a Catholic church building is the house of God. Everything in the church leads us to love and praise him. When you come into church there is a holy water font. The water in the font is blessed. We use this for making the sign of the cross and to remind us of baptism. The most important piece of furniture in the church is the altar. It is the blessed place where the priest stands. It reminds us that Jesus invites us to eat his own Body and Blood at this table. The tabernacle is a holy

container, which is the home of Jesus present in the Blessed Sacrament. There is always a red vigil light, called a sanctuary lamp, next to the tabernacle. There are many beautiful Catholic churches to visit. When you go to visit, remember to say a prayer in front of the Blessed Sacrament near the vigil light.

Worship

The First Commandment tells us to worship God, not anyone else. We worship God by praying in groups like at Mass, or by ourselves.

We can also worship God by singing, doing penance and just doing the right thing. Some good things we do to worship God are sharing, giving things to people who need them, being kind to people and treating everyone the right way. We are always worshiping God when we are doing the right thing.

When we worship together, there are different ways to pray besides the Mass. Here are some of those special ways Catholics have to honor God.

STATIONS OF THE CROSS

In most churches, we find the Stations of the Cross. These are fourteen pictures that show what happened when Jesus was walking to the top of the hill to die on Good Friday. None of them were pleasant for Jesus. (Some churches have a fifteenth picture which shows the resurrection of Jesus.)

During Fridays in Lent, we have special services to pray the Stations together. Praying the Stations of the Cross often includes the traditional song that goes like this:

At the cross her station keeping,
Stood the mournful Mother weeping,
Close to Jesus to the last.

These are meditations we wrote for the fourteen stations.

1. Jesus is condemned to death on the cross.
    The Romans thought Jesus had too much power, and they were afraid of him. Pilate told the soldiers to crucify Jesus.

2. Jesus accepts his cross.
    When Jesus took up his cross, it was maybe twice as big as he was. It was so heavy he could barely carry it.

3. Jesus falls the first time.
    When Jesus fell, it wasn't like when you fall on the cement. He fell and then was crushed by the heavy cross. His back was bleeding from the scourging and the cross put splinters all over his body, in his shoulders, neck, back, and hands.

4. Jesus meets Mary.
    While he was carrying the cross, he saw his mother. You know how when you get hurt your mom gets upset over it? Imagine how she would feel if she

saw you carrying the heavy cross to your death!

5. Simon carries the cross for Jesus.
    Simon was coming home from work. He was tired, and he wanted to get home to his wife. All of a sudden, he finds himself carrying the cross of Jesus. He probably didn't want to help Jesus, but he did it anyway, maybe because the soldiers would have killed him if he didn't.

6. Veronica wipes the sweat off Jesus' face.
    Veronica had the courage to go against what everybody else was doing, and go to wipe Jesus' face. God rewarded her by imprinting an image of Jesus' face on the cloth that she used.

7. Jesus falls the second time.
    This time Jesus could hardly lift the cross off himself, but he did for our salvation. Now he hardly has any flesh left on his back and on his shoulders. Can you imagine how much that hurt?

8. Jesus meets the weeping women.

There were women along the path who were crying because they felt so bad for Jesus. When he met the weeping women he said, "Weep not for me, but for yourselves and for your children."

9. Jesus falls the third time.

This time the guards see that Jesus will die before he gets to Calvary, so they lift the cross off him until he stands up. Jesus begins the exhausting journey again.

10. Jesus is stripped of his clothes.

When they stripped Jesus, the blood from his back had made a scab that glued his tunic to his back. But the soldiers ripped his clothes off. Have you ever pulled off a scab? Imagine now having your back ripped off.

11. Jesus is nailed to the cross.

You know the two-inch nails at the hardware stores? Those were puny compared to the nails that they used on Jesus. The nails that were used on Jesus were eight or nine inches long, and were pounded into the bottom of his hands and into his feet.

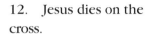

12. Jesus dies on the cross.

Jesus died from the loss of blood and extreme suffering. When the soldier pierced his side for his fifth wound, blood came out with water. Jesus shed ALL his blood for us.

13. Jesus is taken down from the cross.

When they took Jesus down from the cross, Mary wept bitterly. Pretend you had a son that you had loved for thirty-three years. Now pretend he is dead.

14. Jesus is laid in the tomb.

They laid Jesus in the tomb and rolled a large boulder across the entrance. Then they left, feeling very empty and sad. They would have to wait for the Good News of Jesus' resurrection.

We can make the Stations of the Cross as a group on Fridays in Lent. But we can also meditate on the Stations any time we want to by ourselves in church or at home.

EUCHARISTIC EXPOSITION AND ADORATION

Eucharistic exposition is a time when a large consecrated Host, which is the Body of Jesus, is displayed for everyone to see and worship. During exposition the Host is displayed in a special holder called a monstrance. The monstrance is usually placed on the altar. The practice of exposition began in the Middle Ages. Today there are special rules for displaying Jesus in the Blessed Sacrament for a certain amount of time. Eucharistic exposition is very special.

We begin exposition with a song. The priest or deacon uses incense. Incense helps us remember that our prayers rise to God. Next there is usually a reading from the Bible. We can then spend time praying out loud or silently.

Personal silent prayer in front of Jesus in the Blessed Sacrament is called *Eucharistic adoration*. Some parishes have adoration chapels or special times for Eucharistic adoration. Have you ever wanted to feel closer to God? Eucharistic adoration is a time that you can! When you go to adore Jesus in the Blessed Sacrament you can love him and talk to him in a very special way. During adoration, people pray to Jesus. Sometimes they ask him to help them in their troubles, or they pray for their departed loved ones. Sometimes they like to pray the rosary, or just tell Jesus whatever is in their hearts.

When you go to adoration, you might like to just sit quietly and listen to God talking to you. Jesus likes it when we talk to him, but he also wants to speak to us too. While you're at adoration you should try to concentrate on God and not on anything else, no matter how hard it is, so that you feel close to Jesus. You can see him present right before you! Adoring God is wonderful!

EUCHARISTIC BENEDICTION

At the end of the time of exposition we may have Eucharistic Benediction. This is when the priest gives us a blessing by making the sign of the cross over us with the monstrance holding the Host. After this we may say a prayer called the "Divine Praises" that starts out with "Blessed be God, blessed be his holy name...." At the end of the service we sing another song to praise and thank Jesus. The priest or the deacon takes the Host out of the monstrance and places It back in the tabernacle.

There's so much to write about!

Authors take time out for a break

CELEBRATING THE FIRST FRIDAYS

Many Catholics have the custom of receiving Holy Communion on the first Fridays of nine months in a row. We do this to honor the Sacred Heart of Jesus. This custom began when Jesus made a promise to Saint Margaret Mary Alacoque back in the 1600s. Jesus loves us so much. He told Saint Margaret Mary that anyone who made the "First Fridays" would not die in sin or without the sacraments. Many Catholic churches have a special Mass honoring the Sacred Heart of Jesus on the first Friday of the month.

CELEBRATING THE FIRST SATURDAYS

In our Catholic Church we also have the custom of honoring Mary's Immaculate Heart on the first Saturday of the month. When Mary appeared to the three children at Fatima, Portugal, in 1917, she asked people to go to confession and re-

ceive Communion on the first Saturday of the month for five months in a row. She also wants us to recite and meditate on the five glorious mysteries of the rosary on these days. Some Catholic churches have a special Mass honoring Mary to celebrate the first Saturday of the month.

THE ROSARY

The rosary is one of the best prayers that honors Mary. It is made up of fifteen mysteries. They are divided into three groups: the joyful mysteries, the sorrowful mysteries and the glorious mysteries. There are five mysteries in each group.

The joyful mysteries begin with the Annunciation, where Gabriel the angel tells Mary she will have a baby. The second mystery, the Visitation, is where Mary visits her cousin Elizabeth to tell her the good news and to help her. The Nativity is the third mystery and is the scene where Jesus is born in the stable. The fourth mystery is when Mary and Joseph present Jesus in the temple, according to Jewish custom. The fifth joyful mystery is when Jesus is twelve years old and gets lost in a crowd. Mary and Joseph finally find him in the temple.

The sorrowful mysteries help us to remember sad things that happened to Jesus. The first sorrowful mystery is when Jesus is praying after the Last Supper. This is called the Agony in the Garden. The second mystery is when Jesus is tied to a pillar and is getting whipped. The Crowning with Thorns, the third mystery, is when the guards lay the thorns on Jesus' head and mock him, calling him "King of the Jews." The Carrying of the Cross is the fourth sorrowful mystery when Jesus carries the cross up the hill. The last sorrowful mystery is called the Crucifixion. In the crucifixion Jesus is nailed to the cross.

The glorious mysteries are the powerful, miraculous, triumphant times in the lives of Jesus and Mary. The first of the five mysteries is the Resurrection of Jesus, when he rose from the dead on the third day. In the second mystery, the Ascension, Jesus rises up to heaven. The third glorious mystery is Pentecost, when the Holy Spirit came down upon Mary and the apostles. The fourth is the Assumption, when Mary is taken into heaven, body and soul. The Coronation is the last glorious mystery, when the Virgin Mary is crowned Queen of Heaven.

These are the fifteen mysteries of the holy rosary. Some people pray all fifteen every day, but usually just five at a time. We pray the joyful mysteries on Monday, the sorrowful on Tuesday, the glorious on Wednesday. Then we start all over again and say the joyful on Thursday, the sorrowful on Friday (when Jesus died), and the glorious on Saturday. Sundays rotate with the seasons. From Advent to Lent we pray the joyful mysteries. During Lent we pray the sorrowful mysteries, and from Easter to Advent we pray the Glorious.

Sometimes people just rattle off their prayers. Other times they think or meditate about each mystery and story in the life of Christ and Mary. The best way to pray the rosary is to try and think about each mystery as you pray.

NOVENAS

A novena is a special prayer for a special occasion. It takes nine days of prayer to make a novena. It may be prayed in a church, but most of the time people usually pray it in their home. A long time ago, it was prayed for a dead person. Now we usually say a novena for a feast day or for a special request.

VOTIVE CANDLES

Votive candles are the small candles that burn in front of the statue of the Blessed Mother and the other saints' statues or pictures that you may see in your church. (Some churches have electric votive lights.) The beginning of this custom is not known. It started sometime in the Middle Ages and we still do it today. The candle represents the sacrifices that Jesus made for us. In the Middle Ages, people lit candles to remember the different saints. Now we light them when we want Jesus, Mary or the saints to grant us a blessing, or want to show them that we are grateful. A lit candle is a symbol or sign of our prayer.

MEDITATION

Meditation is a kind of prayer in which we mainly use our mind. What you really do is just think about God. You try to make up your mind about things like faith, love and God. Lots of people meditate and try to find the best ways to live their lives and be more like God. Long ago whole groups of people in monasteries meditated. Saint Ignatius had one way to meditate by singing and then being very silent. Saint Sulpice had another way to meditate by reading prayers or Bible stories.

Gregorian chant is becoming popular again. It started back in the Middle Ages. It is words sung in one voice to help empty your mind for holy meditation. Sometimes Gregorian chant is called Plainsong.

We hope that after meditating you will be able to say prayers aloud and from your heart.

SACRAMENTALS

What are sacramentals? Sacramentals are special objects that are blessed by a priest, bishop or Pope. This object needs to represent something holy. Sacramentals are not superstitious or magical charms. They inspire us to pray, but we don't pray to them.

If a sacramental breaks and can't be used, we bury it in the ground or burn it in a fire, because it has been blessed and is holy. Some examples of sacramentals are holy water, statues, religious medals, palms, and ashes.

Holy water reminds us always to be spotless and good. It also symbolizes how Jesus washed the apostles' feet. We use holy water to bless ourselves, especially when we enter or leave church.

The artwork in Catholic churches is blessed, and is a sacramental. Statues remind us of important saints, and help us pray for different things.

There are many different types of religious medals. They usually have pictures of Jesus or Mary or a particular saint on them.

We receive ashes on our foreheads on Ash Wednesday. The ashes are a sign that we are very sorry for our sins. Palms are distributed on Palm Sunday. Some people fold their palms into a cross to remind them of Jesus' love for us. The next year the palms are burned, and that is where we get the ashes for Ash Wednesday.

Bishop Gomez blessing the authors' sacramentals

Many Catholics wear a blessed crucifix or carry a rosary with them as their special sacramental. A cross and a crucifix seem the same, but a cross is plain. A crucifix has an image of Jesus' body on it.

Incense is also a sacramental. It is used by the priest or deacon to bless people or objects. When lit it gives off a special smoke and fragrance that smells like perfume.

Sacramentals can also be actions. A sacramental action is a motion done with respect. For instance, the sign of the cross is a sacramental that blesses us and honors the Father, Son and Holy Spirit. We make the sign of the cross to remind us that Jesus died to save us. The Father is at the top, the Son is in the middle and the Holy Spirit is on the sides.

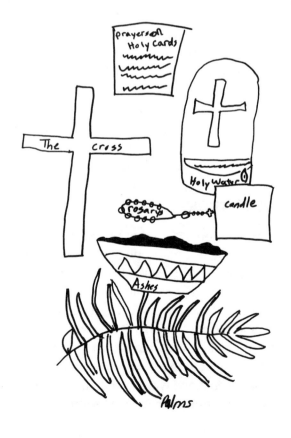

Another sacramental action is genuflecting. This is both an act of adoration and respect that we make to Jesus present in the Blessed Sacrament.

We make a genuflection by kneeling down on our right knee before we enter the pew in church. It is a joy when you are young, but when you get old it is hard to genuflect because your knees get cramps.

Young authors display their different sacramentals

One more sacramental action is kneeling. Kneeling is something that shows reverence to God. It pleases God very much.

Sacramentals and sacraments are not the same thing. Lots of people get these mixed up. A sacramental is an object created by the Church to obtain grace from God. A sacrament is a sign instituted by Christ to give grace. Examples of sacraments are Baptism, Holy Communion, and Confirmation. Sometimes people give us sacramentals when we receive these sacraments.

Some of our authors wrote about their favorite sacramentals:

"My most precious sacramental is a statue of Saint Francis of Assisi. I got it from my godmother for my eleventh birthday. It's about five inches tall and an inch or two wide and plain white. Can you tell why I like it so much?"

"My favorite sacramental is a white rosary I got from my mom and dad on my First Communion. I got it blessed by Father Mel. It is very special."

"One of my sacramentals is a rosary my grandmother got for me. Also I got a cross on a chain from the Mass all the fifth graders went to at the cathedral. The archbishop blessed them for us."

"My favorite sacramental is a crucifix I got for my First Holy Communion. It was blessed by a priest named Father Gerard. He helped my pastor with his work."

DIFFERENT TYPES OF PRAYER

There are four different types of prayer that we use: praise, petition, sorrow and thanksgiving. People speak to God through prayer and God speaks back. Prayer guides our spiritual life. The family is the number one place where we should learn to pray. Priests, teachers and prayer groups can give us more directions for our prayers. There are different places where we can say the prayers we learn, like churches, family rooms, bedrooms, and even monasteries. Sometimes people go on a pilgrimage or retreat to pray and meditate. Keeping quiet gives us time to listen to God better, so we can respond to him in our lives.

Prayer of Praise

A praise prayer is a prayer used to show how happy we are to be loved by God. It is a prayer to let God know we think he deserves our praise. We give praise to our God because we love him. When a baby is born or someone gets married, we are happy people, so we might sing to give praise. Psalms are a kind of song prayer that give praise to God.

We give praise at home when we say our blessings at meals or when we say our prayers at night. We give praise when someone recovers from a car accident or illness.

We give praise at Mass every week, especially on holy feast days all year. We give

praise when anything good happens to us. There are lots of ways to praise in prayer.

We praise God in prayer. We praise him in our actions. We can praise God all day long!

Act of Love

(A prayer that praises God)

O my God, I love you above all

things with my whole heart and soul, because you are all good and worthy of all my love. I love my neighbor as myself for the love of you. I forgive all who have injured me, and I ask pardon of all whom I have injured.

Prayer of Petition

A petition is a serious request that is meant to persuade someone, like your parents, teachers or even God, to give you something. Sometimes it is a written request, like a letter. Sometimes we even ask Mary, Joseph or other saints to pray for us to God.

God, please help my Aunt get well.

When we petition we ask for strength, things we want, or things we need help with. Have you asked for something from your mom or dad? We have all made petitions. Sometimes we get what we ask for, but sometimes we don't. Even then, we still ask for things. If you want help with a test or homework, you ask God for help. Remember that when we ask God for something, we show we believe in him.

We know that God will hear our prayers and will answer them in the way that's best for us. The prayer can be words or just thoughts like, "God, help me so I can pass the fifth grade." When one of our friends was little she had heart surgery and her parents asked God to help her. Then she had the strength to get better! We pray when we think we're not big enough, smart enough, or strong enough to do things by ourselves.

There are many stories in the Bible about petitions. Jonah wanted to get out of the whale, Moses asked for help to get out of Egypt, and little David asked for God's help to defeat the giant Goliath. God heard their prayers of petition and he answered them.

But sometimes God answers our prayers in a way that's different from what we'd like. That's the reason why Jesus taught us to say in the Our Father "Thy will be done."

Prayer of Sorrow

What is a prayer of sorrow? Sorrow is deep concern or worry. Sometimes you apologize because you feel guilty when you have kicked or hit someone, even if it was only in fun. Sorrow is also a cause of trouble and suffering for people. When we are sad we show that we are sorry by saying prayers of sorrow. One time of great sorrow was when Jesus died. When Lazarus died there was great sorrow, and

even Jesus cried. There are so many different people in the Bible who said prayers of sorrow.

We can always pray and feel better when we are worried or some trouble is bothering us. Trouble and pain are part of life. We have sorrow when something hurts us or changes our lives for the worse. Catholics have great sorrow when they think about Jesus dying on the cross. People could not have the chance to go to heaven unless Jesus died, but his death still makes us sad.

Sorrow can be a good thing. It can help us remember the good times.

If you do not study for a spelling test and get a bad grade, your parents will be upset. The next time you will study and get an A+.

When people are sad, they cry and feel lonely. Then they remember to pray.

Pray whenever you are suffering. Pray in the morning, or pray in the evening. Pray when you are sorry. Make up a prayer of sorrow or pray the traditional Act of Contrition. Just do it! God will hear everything in your prayer!

Act of Contrition

O my God, I am heartily sorry for having offended you, and I detest all my sins because of your just punishments, but most of all because they offend you, my God, who are all good

and deserving of all my love. I firmly resolve, with the help of your grace, to sin no more and to avoid the near occasions of sin. Amen.

What We Are Sorry For

I am sorry for being jealous.
I am sorry for stealing.
I am sorry for missing Mass.
I am sorry for lying.
I am sorry for using God's name in vain.
I am sorry for teasing people.
I am sorry for betraying God.
I am sorry that I am not able to forgive as easily as I should.
I am sorry for sinning and being mad at people after they ask for forgiveness.
I am sorry for fighting.
I am sorry for being mean to my little brother or sister.
I am sorry for being disobedient.
I am sorry for talking back to my parents.

God, please forgive all my sins.
Help those whom I've hurt.
Help them to forgive me.
Help me grow closer to your light.
And help me to know your love.

Prayer of Thanksgiving

What is a prayer of thanksgiving? It's a prayer of appreciation or thanks. It should be said whenever we want to say thanks. It is also a way to show we know and celebrate the kindness of God.

We should always be grateful to God for the things we receive. We give thanks to God when a baby is born. We give thanks for our parents. We give thanks to God at our meals. We give thanks when we receive the Eucharist, which is the Body and Blood of Christ. "Eucharist" even means Thanksgiving! The Mass and the Eucharist are a thanksgiving for us all.

Why do we say prayers of thanksgiving? We say these prayers when we are thankful for something. We give thanks to God when nice things happen to our family. We also give thanks to our friends and teachers for their help. We should always give thanks to everyone who helps or gives us something, especially God. He makes all things happen. When we are thankful, we show our love for God.

A Thanksgiving Poem

Thank you, Lord, for my house, where I
will not get wet when it rains.
I can sleep in my bed and I have
privacy and peace of mind.
Thank you, God, for my mom. She
cares for me.
Thank you, God, for my dad. He studies
with me.
Thank you, Lord, for you. You love me.
Thank you for my life. I can run okay.
My brain works fine because you love
me. You helped me grow.

What We Are Thankful For

I am thankful for the love of my
family.
I am thankful for my mom and dad
and food.
I am thankful for having a life to live.
I am thankful for having my dog.
I am thankful for being able to come
to this writers' workshop.
I am thankful for God's love and care.
I am thankful for a wonderful home
with anything I will ever need.
I am thankful for my friends.
I am thankful for having brothers and
sisters.
I am thankful for everything.
Always give thanks.

Lord Jesus,
I'm so glad you're in my life.
If you were not in my life,
I would die.
My love for you, O Lord is true,
True for you!
I love you, O Lord!

The Mass has all four types of prayer in it. So does the Our Father, the prayer that Jesus taught us himself. Can you identify the parts that are praise, petition, sorrow and thanksgiving?

The shortest and easiest prayer of all is "Amen." It means truly, certainly, I believe. When we say "Amen," we are saying positively, absolutely, "Yes, Lord!"

GOD'S POWERFUL ACTS OF LOVE

Miracles

Miraculous events
That God invents,
Like when he healed little Peter's eyes…
That amazed so many guys!

WHAT IS A MIRACLE?

A miracle is a great and wonderful act of God that helps people believe in him. God is the creator of miracles. God always has a reason for sending miracles. The Old Testament miracles were done to show God's love for his people. They also show that he is all-powerful. The New Testament miracles were performed to show Jesus' love for his people and that he really is God. Miracles are much bigger than any power of nature. God makes miracles to help us understand that he is real and that he is with us. The purpose of miracles is to turn our minds, hearts and souls to him.

OFFICIAL MIRACLES

The Catholic Church can declare something an official miracle if it cannot be explained by any natural or scientific reason. Church experts take a long time to carefully investigate miraculous phenomena. The miracles have to go through many steps and pass hard tests before the Church decides to make them

Sister Illaria (center) telling some young authors about Mother Cabrini

official. This is so we can know for sure that they are real and we can believe in them. To be called "official," miracles have to have happened instantly, perfectly and be lasting.

Prayer is important because in prayer we talk and listen to God. Sometimes we ask God for a miracle. He doesn't always give us exactly what we ask for because it might not be what is best for us. But, God always listens and answers us in a loving way. God likes it when we pray to him because we are showing our love and our trust in him.

All miracles are wonderful! Miracles such as Moses parting the Red Sea, Jesus changing the water into wine, and the resurrection are awesome! Little miracles can make a big difference in many people's lives. Read on to find out about lots of marvelous miracles!

A Eucharistic Miracle

Did you know that God has touched our lives with many Eucharistic miracles? We want to share with you one of these miraculous events that occurred in Italy.

Many years ago, a priest named Father Peter of Prague was having doubts about Jesus' real presence in the Eucharist. He was so worried about this! He decided to go on a pilgrimage to Rome. On the way, he stopped at Saint Christina's Church in Bolsena, Italy to pray and ask God to give him a sign that the Eucharist really is Jesus. Then he celebrated Mass. As he began to say the words of consecration, the Host

started to bleed! The blood dripped onto the corporal (a white linen cloth placed on the altar during Mass). Father Peter carefully wrapped the Host in the corporal and carried it down the steps of the altar. The blood dripped onto the brick stairs. Father Peter cried with joy because God had answered his prayers.

Father Peter ran quickly to the nearby town of Orvieto to find Pope Urban IV. With his head bowed, Father Peter admitted the doubts he had been having, and the Pope forgave him. Father Peter told the Pope all that had happened. Pope Urban had people investigate the miraculous event, then told the bishop to bring the Host and the corporal to Orvieto. The Pope was so excited that he ran and met the bishop at a place called the Bridge of the Sun. As soon as Pope Urban saw the Host and corporal, he reverently knelt down. He was filled with awe, and he

praised and honored Jesus. Then he announced that this was a true miracle.

Pope Urban was so amazed by all of this that he started a feast called Corpus Christi, to honor the Body and Blood of Christ. He asked Father Thomas Aquinas (who later became a saint) to write a special liturgy for this feast.

Today, many people still go to visit Saint Christina's Church in Bolsena to see the place where this miraculous event happened. The steps and stones where the blood had dripped were removed and are now kept in a special place in that church.

In Orvieto a big, magnificent, beautiful cathedral was built to honor Jesus and this miracle. The miraculous corporal is kept in a special place there and is shown at special times.

We think the reason why God made this miracle happen is because he wants us to know that it is really he in the Eucharist giving his life for us. This makes us feel tremendously loved to know that Jesus

wants to give himself to us. We also think two miracles happened at Saint Christina's Church on that day. One was that the Host bled, and the second miracle was that Father Peter began to believe again. What do *you* think?

The Miracle of Our Lady of Guadalupe

One day Juan Diego was walking to a special Mass to honor the Virgin Mary. It was the morning of December 9, 1531, in a small village north of Mexico City. He listened to the birds singing and wind rustling between the trees. When Juan got to the crest of Tepeyac Hill, he heard strange music. It was more than a humming or singing or anything he had ever heard. He heard a woman's voice calling him. Something pulled at his mind, heart, soul, and faith. A young Mexican girl, about sixteen years

*An author reading about
Our Lady of Guadalupe*

old, was standing on the side of the hill. Her clothes were washed in light. "What is it you want, my Lady?" Juan asked.

"Juan, I am Mary, the Mother of God, Queen of Heaven," she replied. Juan then knelt at her feet. "Go tell the bishop to build a church for me on this hill," Mary kindly answered.

Juan went to Mexico City to talk to the bishop, Friar Don Juan de Zumarraga. Juan was scared and nervous when he walked in. But remembering the singing seemed to calm all his nerves and tell him what to say. After he told the bishop everything he had seen on the hill, the bishop told him to come back some other time. Juan went and told Mary that he didn't think the bishop believed him. Mary asked him to try again the next day. Juan did as Mary asked. The bishop asked many questions and wanted answers. Juan answered all of them and the bishop still didn't believe. He wanted a sign from the Mother of God.

Juan told Mary what the bishop said. Mary told Juan to come back the next day and he would have a sign from her. Juan didn't make it the next day because his uncle was sick. The day after that Juan went to get a priest for his uncle. On his way he saw Mary again. He was afraid she would be upset with him for not meeting her the day before. She came to him and asked, "How are you, Juan?" Juan replied, "I am fine, but my uncle is sick. I had to take care of him and couldn't meet you." Mary said, "I know. Your uncle is well again! Go to the top of the hill and pick the roses you will find there." Even though it was the

middle of winter Juan found roses there! Juan brought them to Mary. Mary then arranged the roses, put them in his arms and told him to cover them with his cloak. "Show no one what you have. Go straight to the bishop and show him the roses, for this is my sign," Mary said. "This time he will believe you."

Juan set off right away to see the bishop. Juan went into the bishop's room, bowed to him and said, "This is a sign from Mother Mary." Juan let the roses fall. The bishop gasped and fell to his knees, for there on

Devon White

Juan's cloak was a picture of Mary in great detail. The bishop believed Juan and cried, "Let us start on the church at once!"

When Juan went back to his house, his uncle told him that he had seen the Virgin Mary too. His uncle told Juan that Mary had cured him and that she wanted to have a church built on Tepeyac Hill. About nine months later, the church was done. People began to come from all over to pray in front of the shrine where Juan's cloak with the image of Mary was placed. Once, a boy was brought there. He had a deep cut in his back. The boy was almost dead, but his family prayed to Mary to let him live. A few seconds later, the cut healed. Our Lady of Guadalupe helped everyone.

Over the years the church was rebuilt several times. Today the cloak or "tilma" that Juan wore is in a new basilica (a big church) built at the site. Between fifteen to twenty *million* people visit the basilica every year. It is the most visited shrine to the Virgin Mary in the world.

CANONIZATION MIRACLES

Did you know that along with Jesus and Mary we also have many special friends in heaven that love us and want to help us? They are the saints of course! Everyone that is in heaven is a saint, but when the Catholic Church wants to declare an official saint, faithful people start asking these holy people for miracles. After two

Writing about miracles

miracles are approved by the Church, then this step in the canonization process is complete.

Here is an example of this kind of miracle.

Miracle of Saint Frances Cabrini

A happy, healthy, beaming baby boy was born at the Mother Cabrini Hospital in New York. The year was 1921, and the parents of Peter Smith were overjoyed and thankful to God to have a new baby in their lives. Then a tragic event struck the family. A nurse accidentally put a strong solution of silver nitrate into little Peter's eyes. Silver nitrate was used to clean out any infection from birth. The solution severely burned his corneas, spilled out of his eyes and created scars down his tiny face. Peter was screaming in pain. Once the horrified nurse realized her mistake, she ran to get a doctor. She felt terrible! The doctor came and looked at Peter's eyes. He said that the corneas were damaged be-

yond repair and Peter would be blind for the rest of his life!

The sister superior sent another sister to get a relic, a lock of Mother Cabrini's hair, and she put it on Peter's eyes. She told everyone to pray intensely to Mother Cabrini and ask her to pray to God to heal Peter's eyes. The sisters went to the hospital chapel and prayed for a long time.

The next morning, the doctor came to look at Peter. He examined his eyes and they showed no signs at all of the damage! His eyes were healed! Even the scars on Peter's cheeks were barely visible. The doctor was amazed and said, "The boy can see!" It was a miracle!

Then pneumonia struck and Peter was dancing around in death's footprints. The sisters prayed to Mother Cabrini to send another miracle. Again, Peter was healed. The sisters rejoiced!

When Peter was seventeen years old he traveled to Rome to be at the canonization ceremony for Mother Cabrini. He felt very honored that he had received one of the miracles that helped her to be named a saint.

Peter went into the military service for a while and also became a priest! He celebrated his second Mass, a Mass of Thanksgiving, in the very chapel at the hospital where the sisters had prayed for his miracle twenty-five years earlier. Sister Illaria Povero, from Mother Cabrini's Shrine in Denver, Colorado, came and told us about this miracle. She was actually at Father Peter's Mass of Thanksgiving at that hospital!

Father Peter Smith was a priest in Texas for many years. He was a very holy priest and was dedicated to God's people. He gave his entire life in service to our Lord because he wanted everyone to know about God's love for them. What a miracle, and what a miraculous life!

Working on this chapter

PRESENT DAY MIRACLES

Mr. Zee Ferrufino

A man named Zee Ferrufino had a wonderful son named Robby. Robby was diagnosed with cancer. Mr. Ferrufino was very upset and angry with God. He began to lose his faith. This is his story.

Robby loved baseball, football, soccer and wrestling. He had a positive attitude and a strong faith in God. When Robby was seven years old he came home with a pain in his left side. His dad thought it was probably from wrestling. The next day Robby said it still hurt. Therefore, Mr. Ferrufino took him to Children's Hospital. When they got to the hospital the doctors said Robby had to have surgery. After five hours of surgery, Robby's parents were very worried. Finally, during the sixth hour, the doctor came out and told them

Robby with a special friend—G. W. Bailey

the bad news. Robby had cancer in his spleen. When Robby's father heard the news he lost his faith in God. He reasoned, how could a little kid get cancer? He thought only elderly people got cancer. Robby was still hopeful. He still wanted to go to school and he still wanted to play with his friends.

Very early one morning, three years after the sad day they learned of the cancer, Robby called out for his parents. They rushed into his room. Mr. Ferrufino picked him up and Robby died in his arms. Mr. Ferrufino was very sad about Robby dying. He told his employees at his furniture store not to call him unless it was an emergency.

Later that same morning one of Mr. Ferrufino's employees found a dove inside the store. The beautiful white bird had entered the store and begun to fly

Mr. Ferrufino speaking at the writing workshop

around inside. Next, the dove sat down on the cash register, which was Robby's favorite place to sit. The dove refused to fly to the workers and would not leave the store. The employees were afraid that the dove would activate the alarm system so they telephoned Mr. Ferrufino telling him about the dove. He went to the store to see what was going on. When Mr. Ferrufino arrived at the store, the dove flew gracefully into his arms. He took it home in a box and put it in the garage.

The next day when Mr. Ferrufino walked into the garage, the dove flew to him. When Mr. Ferrufino let it outside, the dove flew in circles. Mr. Ferrufino watched as it disappeared into the sky. Mr. Ferrufino believes that the beautiful and amazing dove was a sign from his son! Robby was in heaven with Jesus, he believed, and Mr. Ferrufino would see him again someday. Because of the miracle, Mr. Ferrufino's faith was restored and once again he felt at peace.

Mr. Andres Galarraga

Andres Galarraga is devoted to prayer and his Catholic religion. Mr. Galarraga plays baseball with the Atlanta Braves. During the 1999 baseball season, Mr. Galarraga was diagnosed with cancer.

Because of his love and devotion to Mary, someone suggested that Mr. Galarraga buy white roses to honor her.

He went out and bought four dozen orange roses because he couldn't find any white ones. Then, amazingly, three dozen of the orange roses turned white. His wife crushed some of the white petals and spread them on his back as a way to try to help him through his illness. Mr. Galarraga put his trust in Mary to pray for him and cure him of his cancer.

One night, Mr. Galarraga had a dream that God carried him from his living room to his bed. Then God touched him and his cancer was cured. When Mr. Galarraga woke up from his dream, he was soaking wet. He felt as if someone had thrown water on him.

Mr. Galarraga knows that through the help of Mary he is now healthy and able to play baseball again. Tests done by his doctor in December of 2000 show he has been cured of cancer. He strongly believes he has been cured because of his positive attitude and his prayers to the Virgin Mary, Mother of God. Mr. Galarraga honored Mary by painting a picture of her.

Mr. Jerry Drumm

"You have six months to live." That line to Jerry Drumm changed everything.

When we heard the story of this man we could see the faith pouring out of him. His troubles started in the 1980s

Caitlin Connelly

Mr. Drumm sharing with some of the young authors

when a business he owned was stolen by his best friends. It cost Jerry's family their house, cars, everything. It was terrible. They had to live in his parents' garage until they got back on their feet. During this time Jerry was filled with anger and hate towards everyone. At a mission at church the leader asked everyone to pray for the thing they wanted the most. Jerry prayed for Jesus to be back in his life because he was losing faith in the Lord.

One day Jerry was in his bedroom. His ear hurt so much that it made him pass out. His wife came home and took him to the doctor. The doctor said he had to go to the hospital. When they got there Jerry went into respiratory arrest. The doctor had to make a hole in his throat to put in a breathing tube. Then the doctor told Jerry he had a cancerous tumor the size of a plum in his throat, which was causing the earaches he was having. There was nothing they could do for the tumor. He had about six months left in his life.

Jerry could not sleep that night. Even though he was losing faith he still prayed to God to take care of his family. He also prayed for his friends who had stolen his business. Later he told God that he didn't know how to die. He never asked God to heal him, but only to heal his heart and to remove his hate and anger.

The next day Jerry and his wife were about to pray the rosary. As soon as the rosary touched his hand and he felt the thin, silver, metal cross and beautiful beads, he began to shake and shiver all over, like an earthquake had happened. He felt pin pricks all over his body. He wasn't afraid, but as he continued to lie there he suddenly saw a very bright light. He felt it was the presence of the Holy Spirit. Although he had only gotten a glimpse, he was sure he had seen heaven. He felt completely at home and at peace there.

This experience was a big booster that helped him to have faith in God again. Then Jerry wrote a note to his wife telling her that everything was going to be alright. Two weeks later he could talk again. The first thing he said was to his wife, and it was, "Hey, Baby, how you doing?" Four weeks later Jerry was cancer free. Eight weeks after that he went back to work.

Jerry did not ask God to heal him, but he opened his heart to God. Now he goes to church every Sunday and his faith has fully come back. He is now closer to God. To this day he is free of cancer and his faith is renewed.

The Miraculous Staircase

In September of 1852, the Sisters of Loretto started to travel to the Southwest to educate the people of Santa Fe, New Mexico.

The land was unsettled, so for a while they lived in a very small adobe house. Soon, it became obvious that if the nuns were going to teach the people of Santa Fe they needed a convent and a school. Carpenters were hired to begin construction of the school.

The new school was called Loretto Academy of Our Lady of Light. In 1873, the sisters had a wonderful chapel built in this small community. The church was 25 feet by 75 feet, with a height of 85 feet. The chapel was dedicated to Saint Joseph.

Upstairs in the church the carpenters built a choir loft. But they made a huge mistake! The loft was too high for a ladder and too steep to put in a diagonal staircase. And so there was no stairway that connected the sisters' chapel to the choir loft. All the sisters prayed a novena to Saint Joseph for days on end asking for help. Finally, their prayers were answered!

A gray-haired man riding on a donkey appeared out of nowhere. He offered to build stairs in the new chapel. The only tools he had with him were a saw, a hammer and a T-square. Six to eight months later, the man completed an amazing spiral staircase. The staircase made 360 degree turns, yet it did not have a supporting pole down the center. When the sisters went to pay him, he had disappeared.

Architects came to see this wonder and found that it was not made with nails, only wooden pegs. The architects discovered that the wood used to build the strange staircase did not come from New Mexico. Architects say that the staircase should have crashed to the ground as soon as someone stepped on it. However, it has been used daily for over 120 years. To this day, the nuns believe it was Saint Joseph who built the wonderful circular stairs.

Father Jim Mason

Jim Mason wanted to be a priest more than anything. When he was studying to become a priest at the North American College in Rome, he found out that he had a horrible allergy to wheat. This allergy is called Celiac Disease. If he ate even the tiniest bit of wheat, he would get seriously sick. This was especially terrible news for him because the hosts to be consecrated at Mass are made from wheat!

When Jim was in Rome, he helped at a Mass where he met the sisters of the Missionaries of Charity (the community of sisters that Mother Teresa started). When the sisters found out he had Celiac's, they gave him a relic of Mother Teresa. Then they prayed hard asking her to obtain a miracle for him. The next time Deacon Jim went to have tests done to see how bad his allergy was, the doctors told him that there was no sign of Celiac's Disease anymore!

As you probably have already guessed, Jim is now FATHER Jim Mason. He was ordained a priest on June 22, 2001. To this day, he believes that Mother Teresa touched him with a miracle. Father Jim has even written a letter to the committee working on the canonization of saints. He hopes they can use this evidence for her canonization process.

Weren't these miracles awesome? As you can see from the stories in this chapter, God loves us so much he would do anything for us! Miracles really are great gifts from God that show he really loves and cares for us. Miracles can be anything ranging from seeing our Blessed Mother Mary, or being cured from cancer or other diseases, or becoming closer to God.

God answers all of our prayers in some way and always gives us what we need. When God sends miracles, they help us to learn more about him and we come to know and love him better. Miracles are wonderful because they give us hope and trust that we will live forever with God.

Miracles are happening all the time! Sometimes they are big ones like the ones you read about here, but lots of times they are small ones. So be on the lookout because a miracle may just happen to you!

Father Jim celebrating his first Mass

GOD IS CALLING

A vocation is a call from our Lord
From which we will not be bored.
It is something very important you see,
For it involves your destiny!

Have you ever wondered what it would be like to be married and have a family? Have you ever wondered about what it's like to be a single person? Have you ever thought about becoming a priest, or a brother or a sister in some religious order? Priests and men and women religious believe that the Lord has chosen them to do a special work in the world. Whether a person is called to the married or single life, to take vows in religious life, or to be a priest, it's called a vocation.

Everyone has a vocation. A vocation is a calling or purpose we have in life. Some of us are called to be married. Some are called to be single. But we are ALL called to LOVE God and one another.

The vocation you probably know the most about is marriage. Married life is a covenant or vow between two people to love, honor and cherish one another till death do they part. Married life is a vocation, and the sacrament of Matrimony is its beginning. A visible symbol to show this commitment to each other is a ring which the husband and wife usually wear. Our young authors

The vocation to marriage

Photo credit: Rox's Images

Julia

talked to their parents about marriage. They got a lot of the same responses to the questions they asked about marriage. Most of their parents said that they married a person with the same values, and that being Catholic helped them stay close, because they were able to go to church together. Many of them knew their spouses for a long time before they decided to get married.

Everyone lives a single life unless they are called to another vocation. A single vocation means that you are not married and not a priest or religious. People may be single for different reasons. Maybe they haven't found that special someone or maybe the single life is God's plan for them.

Diane is a young single woman. She's the cousin of one of our authors. After college, she started working for an insurance company. Diane enjoys helping others. She is very happy staying single, if that's what God wants for her. She receives a lot of love and attention from her family and friends and goes places with them if she gets lonely. She is always there when others need her to help with homework, and she gives them rides when they need

one. Our author says that she is glad that Diane is not married because if she were, all of her spare time would be devoted to her husband and not to everyone else.

Mary is also single. She teaches first grade. She has taught for a long time. When she was younger, she had always pictured herself married with children. God had other plans for her. God gave her the children she wanted. In fact, he gave her many children to work with each year. Could God have known that she was needed to touch many children

Erin

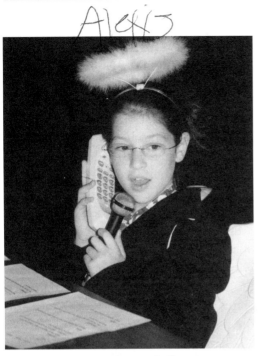

Alexis

*Young author playing God's secretary
in a skit about answering God's call*

instead of just a few? In her free time, Mary enjoys gardening, skiing and spending time with her friends. She is also the godmother of six children!

You know, being single is great too. Remember, Jesus was single!

A vocation to the priesthood or the religious life as a brother or sister is also a call from God. It is an invitation to be close to him in a special way. Priests are called to be ministers of the Church, to celebrate Mass, administer the sacraments and to serve God this way. Some brothers and sisters work to help poor people. Some of them are teachers, others are nurses, community leaders, parish coordinators and missionaries to other countries.

Religious priests, brothers and sisters take vows. The vows they take are poverty, chastity (celibacy) and obedience. The vow of poverty means not having any possessions for themselves. All they have or need is provided by the communities they belong to. The vow of celibacy means that they choose not to marry. The vow of obedience means to promise to listen to and be faithful to the Gospel and always seek God's will, spoken through one's superiors.

God created human beings to love and serve him. The fulfillment of this vocation is eternal happiness. Christ calls all people to be very holy. Priestly, religious,

Michelle Roberts

Student writers working on this chapter

Carolyn
Michelle H.

married and single vocations are all calls to dedicate our lives to the service of God, the Church, and our neighbor.

It would be so cool to have a job where you devote your life to helping people and spreading God's love. Let us introduce you to a few people who've heard and answered this call.

Bishop José H. Gomez

A really neat thing happened during our writing workshop! Newly ordained Bishop José H. Gomez of the Archdiocese of Denver came to visit us.

Bishop Gomez grew up in Monterrey, Mexico. When he was fourteen years old, he felt God calling him to do something special. He took his faith very seriously and learned a lot from the Marist Brothers who taught him in high school. They shared the importance of devotion to the Blessed Mother. When he went to college José was planning to be a businessman. "I wanted to make a lot of money, or be a baseball player," he said. José thought becoming a priest was too hard. He was surprised to find out that God had other plans for him. So, after José graduated from college with a degree in business, he decided to become a priest, and he went to Rome to study theology.

Bishop Gomez was ordained a priest in Spain in 1978. After spending some time with the people of God in Spain and Mexico, Father Gomez came to the United States. He worked in Texas as a priest in the diocese of Galveston-Houston.

When Archbishop Charles Chaput of Denver realized how much the Hispanic population had grown in northern Colorado, he decided to ask Pope John Paul II for another bishop to serve the archdiocese. Archbishop Chaput was asked to turn in three names of his choice to the Holy See in Rome (the Pope and his helpers). They picked out Father José Gomez's name, and so that's how we got him as a second bishop in Denver.

Bishop Gomez was so patient. He answered all the questions we had about the ordination of priests and bishops. He told us that his ordination was the most beau-

Meeting the bishop

Bishop Gomez addressing young authors

tiful celebration he had ever experienced. He said that the priests being ordained lie stretched out on the floor in front of the altar with their hands crossed under their heads to show their unworthiness before God. He said that he remembers praying really hard while he was lying down at his ordination. He told us about the laying on of hands by the bishop and the anointing with oil. He said they used so much oil that it ran down his head. It went into his eyes and over his glasses. He said, "There was so much oil on my glasses that I hardly could see."

Bishop Gomez enjoys sports, reading and driving in the car. He told us that taking a drive relaxes him. The Green Bay Packers used to be his favorite football team. He liked them because they were the best team when he was a young boy.

Bishop Gomez likes celebrating Mass and being with people the most. When he got the phone call saying that he was going to be made a bishop, he asked if they were talking to the right person. Then he went right to the chapel to pray and ask God to give him the grace to serve the people well as their bishop.

At the end of his talk, Bishop Gomez told us a little riddle. It goes like this: "Do you have one? Do you carry it with you? And do you use it? There's only one answer: the rosary."

We are so glad Bishop Gomez is a U.S. citizen and is here with us in Colorado. Maybe he'll become a Bronco fan now!

Father Francis Gloudeman, O. Praem.

Father Francis

Being sick isn't fun, but visiting with Father Francis can make it better. One of our authors, John Lilles, was very sick and in a California hospital. One afternoon his dad told him that a priest wanted to hear his confession if that was okay with him. At first, John was very shocked to hear that a priest rode a bicycle to the hospital just to see him. John talked to Father Francis and thought he was very kind. Father Francis is known as the "Bicycling Priest" because he travels by bicycle and even rides a unicycle sometimes.

Father Francis is a Norbertine priest. The Norbertines have a great love for the Holy Eucharist. They teach and pray and want to be good examples to one another and to other priests.

Father Francis's job is to teach religion to homeschooled children in Orange County, California. He teaches 160 children ages six to seventeen about their faith and about Jesus and the Church.

Father Francis has wonderful memories of holidays with his family. When he was younger he wanted to be a policeman, fireman, garbage man or soldier. It was during his junior year in high school that he heard God calling. Father Francis is very prayerful and has a great devotion to our Lady. When asked if he had any heroes, he said that he had more than one. When he was little, his dad was his hero. When he was a young man, Father Leo Celano and Father Luke Zimmer were his heroes. Now that he is an adult, his hero is Jesus.

While Father Francis was studying in Rome his community was asked to provide altar servers for Pope John Paul II. Francis was chosen to hold the book because he was short, just like the Pope. It was an honor to be in the presence of a living saint.

Father Francis told us another story, about how God answers children's prayers. An eight-year-old girl and her family prayed for their grumpy mailman. The family prayed so hard and God soon heard their prayers. While Father Francis was visiting one day he had a chance to talk to the grumpy mailman. Guess what happened!? The both of them got along so well that Father Francis got to hear the mailman's confession on the little girl's front porch. The mailman has gone back to church and isn't grumpy anymore.

Father Francis Gloudeman playing his accordion as he rides!

Father gave up his car and has traveled over 31,000 miles on his bike, homeschooling and visiting sick kids. While traveling on his bike he prays the rosary using the rosary ring that he wears on his finger.

Father Jeff Wilborn

Jeff thought that the people he read about in the Bible were weird. He thought that being a priest was a silly job! He started laughing when he heard people talking about being a priest. He wanted to be an Air Force pilot. But God had a different idea.

Jeff owned a motorcycle and he bought a radar detector in order to know if the police were trying to catch him speeding. One day he was riding on his motorcycle paying attention to his new toy and not paying attention to the road. He didn't notice a car in front of him. When he saw the car, it was too late to stop, so he closed his eyes and hung on to his motorcycle. He took a flip over the car and hit his shoulder on its roof. When Jeff had finished his "routine," he landed on one foot and one knee —a genuflecting position! When he looked up Jeff saw that his prized motorcycle had been totaled. Jeff asked himself, "Why was I spared?" He won-

Father Jeff Wilborn

dered if maybe God had something better in mind for him.

Jeff grew up in Aurora, Colorado. He was not a Christian and never went to church. He had a Catholic friend, Dan, whom he knew from kindergarten. Dan wanted Jeff to convert to Catholicism, so he began trying to get Jeff to start going to church. Jeff wouldn't go. But deep down, Jeff felt something going on, something mysterious.

About one year after his motorcycle accident, Jeff asked Dan if he could go to church with him. After the first time going to church, Jeff felt a little peaceful inside, so he kept asking to go to church with Dan. Soon it became a regular routine. Dan even let him have his Bible to study. Later, when Jeff decided to become a Catholic, he went to RCIA (Rite of Christian Initiation for Adults) classes. After a year of studying and being taught about the Catholic faith, he became a Catholic. Can you imagine how his friend

Dan felt when Jeff decided to go to the seminary? After spending many years in Rome studying, Jeff was finally ordained a Catholic priest during the summer of 2000.

Alfred Matayo, Seminarian

Can you imagine being put into jail, beaten terribly, and having everything taken away from you? That is exactly what happened to Alfred Matayo.

When Alfred was young, he heard God calling him to become a priest. He studied and lived in the Sudan, a country in Africa. His country had big problems and his family left because people were killing Christians, and there was a lot of fighting going on.

Alfred stayed because he was going to school to become a priest. His family was very sad because they worried that he might be killed. Alfred moved in with his uncle, who was his only relative in the city.

Then the government closed all the schools. That's when Alfred and twelve other people began walking to Uganda where his mother lived. It was 150 miles away! The group was stopped by police because the police thought they knew information about the country's military. They arrested Alfred and the others and threw them into jail.

In the jail, there were already forty-eight people in the cell. So Alfred and his friends made it sixty-one! The only water that they could have was a leaf dipped in

Alfred Matayo

water and they would have to suck all the moisture out of the leaf. The police took all the money they had. They had very little food, so only eight or ten prisoners would get to eat a day. The first three days in jail, Alfred had nothing to eat at all! When he finally got to eat, he only had half a sandwich. All of the prisoners would have to stand up all day and even sleep standing up! Somebody once came to see if Alfred wanted to leave jail. He said, "No." Alfred would not leave because he did not want to go without the other prisoners.

Alfred and the other prisoners were beaten harshly every day. Sometimes they got electric shocks too. Sometimes they would even get smacked in the head and chest by the soldiers' guns. It was so bad that Alfred thought he was going to die. Alfred and his friends were even forced to confess things that they knew nothing about. It was really tough for him. To help get him through all of this suffering, Alfred prayed every day, especially the rosary.

Alfred finally got out of jail with the help of the governor and bishop. But it was still hard for him because not much was left for him. He only had one shirt and one pair of pants and no money. He was so sick too.

Alfred's parish priest gave him a bag of beans to sell on the street so he could earn some money. The police didn't like that, so they arrested him again! He spent three more days in jail. He was beaten and kicked. Alfred felt so angry. When he got out, his uncle helped him to get over his anger.

Then the government opened up the schools again, and Alfred returned to his studies. But Alfred soon found out that the police wanted to arrest him again. He made plans to escape from the country. First he had to make some money by selling clothes and beer to buy the special papers he needed to escape. The only way he could get out of the country was by pretending to be someone else! Alfred still had a hard time escaping though, because when he got to the airport, he was stopped at the entrance, and his passport was ripped up by the police. When he finally got out of the Sudan and into Ethiopia, he only had twenty dollars to live on. He made it last for a month while he continued trying to leave Africa. He went to Egypt and the Egyptians didn't help him either.

Finally, with the help of some Franciscans from America, Alfred got to the United States! He went to Minnesota where two of his brothers were already living. Alfred found a job at a store and saved money for college. A kind priest helped Alfred get to Saint John Vianney Seminary where he is continuing his studies to be a priest for the Archdiocese of St. Paul and Minneapolis, Minnesota. Alfred Matayo is finally realizing his dream!

Alfred wants to be a priest so he can help people and work for peace and justice in the world. Alfred has suffered greatly in his life, but he feels that it was his Catholic faith that got him through it all. His faith gave him the strength to live in patience. One day Alfred would like to go back to Africa if he can, so he can teach the people there about God. Alfred Matayo is very brave to have endured so much pain and suffering, and we hope he will make it back to Africa one day!

Father Tom Bush

In 1993, the Pope was coming to Denver! It was a really big deal to everyone who was Catholic, and especially to Tom

Tom Bush (at right) helping to build a church in Russia before he became a priest

Bush. Before the Pope came, some sisters asked Tom if he would go to Russia to help build a church. "But the Pope is nearly here!" said Tom. The sisters said that the Pope would come to Latvia, the country closest to Russia, soon. They told Tom that he could see the Pope there. Tom said yes and went to Russia.

The day came for him to get a visa (passport, not a credit card) to Latvia so he could go see the Pope. But only so many visas were given out each day. Tom was told to come back the next day. When he came back, the visa office was not open and the train was going to leave soon, so he just got right on the train. No one checked if he had his visa because our Lord wanted him to see the Pope! He saw the Pope.

When Tom was going back to Russia and they were almost there, the train was stopped by some fierce looking soldiers with machine guns. They asked to see everyone's visa. When they found out Tom did not have one, they told him to get off the train and they guarded him with their machine guns. A boy from Florida said he was going with Tom. Everyone in the train prayed. Then, all of a sudden, all the nuns just jumped up and said, "We are going, too." This frightened the guards so much that they told everyone to get back on the train, even Tom. So, he made it back to Russia for the rest of his stay.

Tom wanted to be a priest and he was ordained in Lincoln, Nebraska, in 1999. He is now Father Tom Bush.

Deacon Sam Lopez

Sometimes a hard beginning makes for a happy ending. When he was a young boy, Sam spent time in an orphanage with two of his three brothers and one of his four sisters. Sam had funny stories to tell about being in the orphanage. One story was about Sister Regina, who would take a group of boys out to the garden she tended. Sam remembers her picking up prickly weeds and throwing the weeds at them! Then they would get to throw them back! She taught the boys to box and to wrestle. She was like a mother to Sam.

Sam had many ideas about what he would be when he grew up. He wanted to be Superman and be like other super heroes. He was an altar boy and even thought he might like to be a priest. He had very loving grandparents, a really nice teacher in the first grade, and Sister Morgan who helped him to become the special man that he is today. Sam Lopez remembers that God was important to him when he was little. So was hard work. He lived with a wonderful foster family he grew to

Deacon Sam Lopez

Deacon Sam works for the phone company. He thinks his job at church is not as important as the time he spends with the people he meets every day. He talks to people about getting back to their own church, whatever their church might be, so they will be close to God. Deacon Sam believes this is the most important reason he is a deacon.

Brother Gary Sawyer, ECSA

Brother Gary Sawyer has done many exciting things as a brother. He recently returned from the Mount Kilamanjaro Region in the country of Tanzania in Africa. While he was there, he and the other brothers helped the local people install

love so much that he decided he wanted to be married and have kids when he grew up. Sam did just that. He has been married over twenty years and has three daughters.

Sam became a deacon when he was a grown-up. A deacon is a man that serves God. Deacon Sam helps the priests at church to make their work easier. He helps at Mass. Sometimes he does the teaching after the Gospel. Deacons can perform three things. They baptize, marry and bury people. Deacons serve people in many different ways.

Deacons can receive all seven sacraments. That is more than a priest because deacons can be married. Deacon Sam has received all seven sacraments, because he has even received the sacrament of the Anointing of the Sick.

Brother Gary at the writing workshop

Brother Gary Sawyer and his 5ᵗʰ grade class

solar panels for electricity. They set up three satellite stations to allow computers to access the Internet and e-mail.

Brother Gary was on the welcoming committee for Pope John Paul II when he came to Denver for World Youth Day. He also took a trip to Rome for World Youth Day there.

Another time, Brother Gary brought a group of young people to Mexico to help build a house. Brother Gary was one of several novices in his group that was invited to the United Nations in New York City to talk about religious life. He has lived in New Jersey, Ohio, Kentucky, Louisiana and Colorado and enjoys his life as a brother.

Before Gary became a brother, he was a teacher of early childhood education. He became a brother to answer God's call. He lives in a house that is very small and quiet and he owns a dog. He likes to play with his dog and enjoys photography, swimming, bicycling and tennis. He does miss having his own children but he says, "That's why God wanted me to be a teacher." His main fear is not teaching children everything he can about the love of Jesus. His normal day is prayer and work, then prayer.

Brother Gary has one brother, one sister and two nieces. They are all happy that he's a brother. He likes being a brother because it shows how he loves

Jesus. Brother Gary took three vows of poverty, chastity and obedience. He isn't ordained and he doesn't give sacraments, but Brother Gary does more stuff with kids than many priests do.

Brother Gary does not wear his habit a lot but wears regular clothes. He usually wears black and gray clothes and a special ring as a sign of his vocation to the the Brothers of Saint Augustine Emmaus Community.

When Brother Gary was a novice, the brothers sent him to Mexico to study Spanish. He was extremely excited because his community does not usually send novices out. When he arrived in Mexico City, he met some of his Mexican brothers who told him he would not be able to study Spanish. Brother Gary was very disappointed because an orphanage really needed him. When they got to the orphanage, there were 500 children and only five brothers. Wow! He was put in charge of 100 kids who did not speak the same language as he did. But after lots of prayer, Brother Gary found a way to communicate with the children and was very happy at the orphanage.

He has been a teacher, a Director of Religious Education, and a consultant for child care programs. Brother Gary was the first Director for African American Ministries for the Archdiocese of Denver.

He would like all kids to know that all of us have a vocation, a calling from God and we just have to listen. He would also like us to know Jesus is everyone's best friend.

Patrick

Brother Simon Dankoski, CFR

Today we saw the coolest video about this brother who can really rap!

Brother Simon Dankoski

His name is Brother Simon. Brother Simon is a member of the Franciscan Friars of the Renewal. Here is his rap about the three vows the Franciscan Friars take:

Poverty, it's about being poor,
Maybe sleeping on the floor, not going
  to the store.
But deep, deep down it's much, much
  more.
Being poor in spirit is loving God to
  the core.

Chastity can be a blast you see,
'Cause you're preparing for the
  marriage of eternity.

*God alone is your spouse, As you're
    building up the house.*
*Your deepest desire, drawing you
    higher and higher.*

Obedience, it ain't convenience.
*Going where you're sent, lett 'in down
    your defense.*
It's a chill pill for the will
Even Jesus obeyed the Father's will.

*Three vows, three ways of Christian
    transformation.*
*One thing—be certain, ... it's a divine
    vocation.*

Matthew Dankoski (who's now known as Brother Simon) was born in Texas on Feb 24, 1976. He has three older brothers and a younger sister. While Matthew was growing up, he liked to fish and camp and even became an Eagle Scout. He loved riding a stunt bike. One time he got into an accident on his stunt bike and he had to have quite a few stitches on his leg. He thought it was great because he was seven and his scar looked like a 7.

Matthew's family was very close and had many traditions. One thing they did was called "the eleven-year-old trip." When one of the kids turned eleven, their dad took just that kid on a special trip. Matthew wanted to go camping and fishing for his trip. This was a special time for his dad to prepare him for his teenage years and teach him more about his responsibilities in the future. Matthew is still very close to his father and respects him for his wisdom.

Matthew's mom kept a diary every day. His mom wrote about the day Matthew was confirmed when he was in tenth grade. She commented that this was the first time she had heard Matthew mention that he wanted to be a priest. When he was eighteen, Matthew visited the Franciscan order for the first time.

"Coraggio," which means "courage" in Italian, has a special meaning for Brother Simon. He remembers the event that made it special. Matthew and several of his classmates from Franciscan University in Steubenville, Ohio, went to Rome to see the Pope. Matthew was selected to present the Pope with a gift from the group. They gave the Pope a picture, a spiritual bouquet and chocolates. The group knew he loved chocolate. Matthew said, "These are for you, Holy Father, coraggio!" Then the Pope answered, "Coraggio!" back. Matthew used his coraggio to enter the Franciscan Friars of the Renewal and become Brother Simon.

Brother Simon dresses a lot like Saint Francis of Assisi who started the Franciscans around the year 1200. His habit has a hood on it that

Checking over the text

is really helpful whenever he wants to have privacy while he is praying. He puts his hood up to cover his head so it will be quiet. Brother Simon also has a rosary attached to the rope that acts as his belt. His rosary has one different colored bead on it. Brother Simon remembers to pray to Simon of Cyrene when he comes to this bead. He chose his name Simon to honor this man who helped Jesus carry his cross.

The Franciscan Friars work together with the Franciscan Sisters of the Renewal. They serve the poor and preach the Gospel. They encourage families to have more faith and help the poor. They collect food and distribute it to families

each week. The Franciscans eat the same food that they distribute to the poor. At Thanksgiving and Christmas they give out about 2,500 baskets of food. One Christmas the brothers and the sisters borrowed some animals from the zoo and put them in the Christmas pageant for the people getting baskets. It made everyone laugh and have a really fun time learning more about Jesus' birth.

Whether spending the night helping at the men's homeless shelter or teaching boys in trouble at Children's Village, Brother Simon is very happy with his decision to serve the Lord and help build the Church. We think God is happy with him too.

Sister Francis Teresa, CFR

Sister Francis Teresa is a member of the Franciscan Sisters of the Renewal. She

Sister Francis Teresa finds real happiness in serving God

lives in a part of New York City called "the Bronx." She wears a one piece gray habit. Sister Francis has a special love for Jesus on the cross and looks like a cross when she holds her arms straight out. When anyone sees her they are reminded of Jesus on the cross. Sister wears a rope around her waist. It has three knots on it. She jokingly said they stand for "no money, no honey and one boss" which are the three vows of poverty, chastity and obedience. Sister Francis also has a

large rosary on the rope around her waist. She calls the rosary her weapon. Another part of her habit is a white veil to show she is a religious person. The veil shows she is consecrated, which means to be set apart for God. Franciscan Sisters of the Renewal never take off their habits except when they shower or sleep. They wear an apron when baking or cooking.

Jennifer O'Donnell, now known as Sister Francis, lived in Colorado, Saudi Arabia and finally Las Vegas, Nevada. She was the youngest of four children and the only girl. Her family went to Mass on Sunday but she rarely studied religion outside of church. Jennifer never thought about being a sister. She liked sports, hiking and camping. In college, she stopped going to church. She kind of gave up God. She was all caught up in studying and parties. Even though she was raised as a Catholic, her faith didn't seem important to her. She was worried about success in the business world. Everything in the world said you needed a car, nice clothes, and friends. She got a job as a financial analyst in a Las Vegas hotel. She had everything she needed in this world. She even owned her own townhouse. But still she felt unfulfilled. Jennifer began to see that financial success was not making her happy. She felt sad and thought she was missing something.

One thing she needed in life was God. Jennifer found he was the missing piece. She started going to church and reading the Bible. She soon realized God gave her everything. She wanted to give him everything in return. Jennifer gave up her job to serve on the National Evangelization Team. She traveled all around the United States sharing the Good News of God with other Catholics. She spoke to young people so they wouldn't make the same mistakes she had made.

When Jennifer was twenty-six, she felt in her heart that God was calling her. She started thinking and reading about religious life and started visiting convents. She noticed that sisters were happy and full of joy and love. They were helping the poor and serving the Lord, just like the apostles.

Soon after, Jennifer gave away her townhouse and most of her clothes. She felt really excited. She entered the community of sisters in September of 2000. She received the habit a few months later at a special ceremony. Sister Francis' hair was long, curly, and beautiful. She cut it and offered it up as a gift to God.

Sister Francis will pray and study to prepare for her vows. After two years she will make her first vows, which she will renew each year for four years. Then she will be able to take her final vows. She will get a ring when she takes her final vows. This ring will show that she's married to Jesus. Every sister is a bride of Christ. When Sister Francis dies she will be buried in her religious habit.

Sister Francis has lots of fun being a sister. When the sisters sit down for dinner, they stay for a long time joking and laughing. The sisters are like a real family. They play guitar together, sing, go to the beach and to the park and also play Frisbee. Once they even went sledding.

Here is some advice Sister Francis gave us: "Don't wait; start believing now. Pray and hear God's voice." She encourages young people to go to Mass, to have good friends around them, and to serve and help the poor.

Sister Dorothy Guadalupe of the Unborn Jesus, SV

When she was growing up, Dorothy used to help her father restore old cars. Today when Sister Dorothy visits her hometown of St. Louis, Missouri, she drives a 1955 Chevy that she restored with her brothers and sisters.

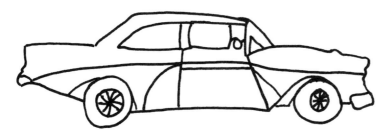

Most of her life Dorothy went to Catholic schools. On her thirteenth birthday her parents gave her a Bible. She began to read the Psalms. She participated in many activities such as Girl Scouts, softball, soccer, field hockey, lacrosse and basketball. When she was young she wanted to be an astronaut or a teacher. While in high school she asked God if she should become a sister and the answer she felt was no.

Dorothy liked math and science enough to go on to engineering school. She studied mechanical engineering in college. She landed a job at NASA (the agency of the government in charge of all the satellites in space) working on the different space shuttles and robotics. She actually worked on building things like robots. It was then she felt God calling her to the religious life. She got involved with pro-life work. After a lot of thought she decided to quit her job at NASA to work full time

with women who were going to have babies.

While she was doing this work with the pregnant women, she got to know about the Sisters of Life. After a while, Dorothy joined them. The Sisters of Life were founded in 1991 by Cardinal John O'Connor in New York City. Sister Dorothy and the other Sisters of Life take care of women who are pregnant. The Sisters of Life spend most of their time praying and promoting the holiness of all life. They don't spend much time watching TV or doing things that do not involve our Lord. Once in a while they do watch G-rated movies (they find all the other ratings offensive). The sisters have fun riding bikes and playing volleyball, but find it hard to play some of their favorite sports like soccer, because of the long habits they wear.

Sister Dorothy's day is very busy. Her day starts at 5:00 A.M. praying for all the unborn children of the world. Sister Dorothy attends Mass with all the other sisters. Then they eat breakfast while one of the sisters reads to them. After breakfast the sisters begin their chores. At 9:00 they begin their apostolic work, which is sort of like community service. Sister Dorothy's apostolic work is to work in a library. At noon they go to the chapel for a midday prayer. They do all of the morning activities in silence. Then at lunch, after their midday prayer, they can talk. (How many of you think you can be silent that long?) After lunch, they have recreation time for one hour and go back to apostolic work. From 4:30–6:00 they pray. They eat dinner in silence while someone reads. At 7:45 they have community recreation.

As you can see, Sister Dorothy and the Sisters of Life spend most of their day in prayer, praying for others and listening to what God has to say to them.

Sister Dorothy believes that children can find their own vocation by becoming quiet and listening to God. She says that the most important thing in her life is her relationship with Jesus. She reminds us that we all have a vocation and each of us is called by God to a special vocation in life. God's plan for us is love. She also reminds us that sisters are normal human beings, who have been touched by God in a special way. The sisters try to live a life like Jesus. Jesus guides all people and watches over them with loving care, and that is what the Sisters of Life try to do.

Sister Joanna Strouse, SDSH

When she was little, Joanna didn't have any idea that she would be a nun when she grew up. In fact, she did not always act like we think a future Catholic nun would, because she often was bored in Mass (just like us kids) and got into fights with her sisters at church. Joanna grew up doing the things that most kids liked to do. When she got to high school she was on the color guard team and performed on the field with the marching band. She was a good student. She would often pray for guidance about what she would do after high school. She thought that she was going to study engineering and physics and after that work in the space program.

Joanna was the oldest of four girls. Her mother was Catholic, but her father didn't have a faith growing up because his dad wouldn't allow it. When Joanna was six, her father was baptized Catholic along with her baby sister. Baptism day was a special day

This takes concentration!

Sister Joanna Strouse (left) enjoys spending time with her sisters

in the Strouse family. Each year on the anniversary of their baptisms, Joanna's parents would light their baptismal candle to celebrate that special day, and have a family dinner together.

Doreen, Joanna's friend and babysitter, had joined the Society Devoted to the Sacred Heart of Jesus and become Sister Doreen. This made Joanna consider becoming a nun. But she had always imagined herself with children. Becoming a nun had never been in the picture.

After visiting her aunt and uncle during her senior year in high school, Joanna came home inspired by their strong religious faith and practice. She knew she needed to pray more. She went to visit with the sisters at the convent. Here she learned that God loved her for who she was and that he had a plan for her. All she

needed to do was ask him what it was. After she came home, she decided to ask God what he wanted for her life. She prayed the rosary, prayed a novena (a group of prayers said for nine days for a special intention) and offered a special prayer to Saint Therese asking for help. Saint Therese has promised to pray to God for us when we ask her for help. Sometimes she sends people roses as a sign that God is answering their prayers. On the very first day Joanna started her prayers, her grandmother gave her a rose. One day the rose was on a stamp she received on a piece of junk mail. But most days the roses were real. She got them for the nine days of the novena and for two more weeks after.

Sister Joanna is now a member of the Society Devoted to the Sacred Heart of

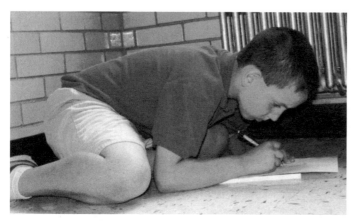

The floor is great for drawing on

Jesus. As a teacher, she is surrounded by the children she had hoped to have. She makes sure the children know that God loves them very much and that "He has a plan to make them their happiest, truest self." The Society Devoted to the Sacred Heart is all about teaching religion to all ages. She loves the family spirit of the community and the way the sisters really love God and each other. "My community is such a gift to me," Sister Joanna says. "I can't imagine living anywhere else."

Sister Anna Truong, FSP

After the Vietnam War ended, many Vietnamese families moved to the United States. They came because Vietnam had become a Communist country and it was hard to make a living and get a good education. In some places Catholics were not allowed to practice their faith. This story tells you about Sister Anna Truong and her journey to the United States and a life of service for the Lord.

In Vietnam Anna lived in the country with her family in a house without electricity. This did not stop her from experiencing the joys of childhood. Many children were not able to play during the day because they went to school or worked in the fields with their parents. So children from the neighborhood flooded into the main street at night to play by moonlight. Anna and her eight brothers and sisters lived with their parents in Vietnam. She has very happy memories of this time in her life.

Anna came from a very religious family. Family holidays like Tet and Christmas were important to the Truong family. Tet is a three-day Vietnamese holiday similar to our New Year's Day celebration. Anna would help her mother prepare for this celebration weeks before. Christmas was a wonderful celebration because the parish organized plays and games. It also presented dances. The Truong family felt prayer was the most important thing to do both morning and night. Anna's father also wanted his children to get a good education.

Anna's older brother was the first to come to the United States. Then Anna's father thought she should come and join him in New Orleans, so she could continue her studies. She came with five more of her brothers. As she was praying, she kept asking herself if she should serve God as a nun. Anna even asked the Lord to send someone to knock on her door and help her make this decision.

The next week, two nuns were visiting families near Anna's neighborhood. They were carrying out their missionary work by bringing people the Word of God. Their car broke down not far from Anna's house and they ended up knocking on her door! Then the two sisters invited Anna to come to a day of recollection at their convent. Anna went. Within the same year she joined these sisters, the Daughters of St. Paul, and became Sister Anna.

Sister Anna Truong puts Jesus on the Web!

The rest of Sister Anna's family moved to the United States in 1991. She sees them whenever she goes to New Orleans for work or when she visits them during her vacation each year. There are other nuns from Vietnam in Sister Anna's order. This is fun because she can speak Vietnamese with them. Many of these sisters came to the States for the same reasons that Sister Anna did.

Have you ever wondered what sisters like best about

being a sister? Sister Anna told us that she feels very happy and content. She lives in Boston, Massachusetts, with a wonderful family of sisters that enjoy what they do and share many good times. They live out their vocation as Daughters of St. Paul where they help spread God's Word through the media. The Daughters of St. Paul publish religious books, tapes and videos. The Daughters of St. Paul printed this book. They are helping us to share our faith with others.

Sister Anna has an exciting job as a Webmaster. This is a person who sets up Web pages online. Sister asked us to encourage you to visit her Web page. It will help you learn more about your Catholic faith. Go to www.daughtersofstpaul.com Check out the kids' section and let Sister Anna know what you think about it.

Sister Anna has a goal to be a saint. We think she will make it!

DISCOVERING YOUR VOCATION

We hope you've enjoyed these stories. Here's a prayer to help YOU decide what to do in your life:

Dear God, help me to see what you mean for me to do in life. Help me to open my heart to your plan for me. Guide me to what will make me happy and please you. Amen.

Things that are good to do to help you discover what your vocation is:

First: You should be quiet so that you can hear when God's calling you. You pray and listen for your answer from him.

Second: Try to find someone that you trust and someone who loves God who will listen to you and answer your questions.

Third: Ask a priest, brother, or sister at your church to introduce you to a vocation director. That is a person who helps you decide what God wants you to do.

Fourth: Read about what God is calling you to.

Fifth: If you feel you are being called to a religious community, write and ask that community any questions you may have.

Sixth: Go and visit the people you feel you have been called to and spend lots of time with them to get to know them better.

Last: Wait and see if your choice makes you as happy as you feel on Christmas morning when all your presents arrive from Santa.

FAITH IN ACTION

God Gave Talent

God had talent and held it in his hand.
He sprinkled it over little babies and
*   each one got some.*
Some use their talent to help
*   another person and show they care.*
If you haven't found it, keep looking, it's there,
Because God gave you talent!

Jesus asks us to take our faith in him and put it into action by caring for others. He told us long ago, when he was here on Earth, that by helping each other we would be helping him. People of many ages are still helping Jesus today by caring for others. God gives us the talents we need to serve others. Jesus also opens doors for us so that we can use all our talents in a kind, loving way.

From the sunny coast of California to the quiet shores of Maine, people are putting their faith into action. Because Catholic churches are all over the world,

Putting our faith into action brings us joy!

Catholics can go almost anywhere to serve God.

In addition to being able to serve all around the world, Catholics can be strengthened almost anywhere, too. God gives us strength when we attend Mass and receive Jesus in Communion. And you can go to Mass in almost any place in the world!

In this chapter you'll learn about many U.S. Catholics today who are putting their faith into action. We decided to use a passage from the Bible to guide our writing and our chapter. If you would like to read it in your Bible, it is in Matthew, chapter 25, verses 34–39 and verse 40.

"Jesus said, '…Come, you who are blessed by my Father. Inherit the Kingdom prepared for you from the foundation of the world. For I was hungry and you gave me food, I was thirsty and you gave me drink, a stranger and you welcomed me, naked and you clothed me, ill and you cared for me, in prison and you visited me'" (Mt 25: 34–36).

"Lord, when did we see you hungry and feed you?" (Mt 25: 37)

Some people give food to the hungry…

All around the world people of many ages are feeding people who can't pay for their own groceries. Saint Sebastian Parish in West Los Angeles, California, for in-stance, has a food pantry. Every Monday people who are having trouble paying for food can come and receive it from the pantry. The groceries are handed out by helpful Catholics.

The pantry is supported by Operation Rice Bowl, an organization that raises money through donations from churches and schools. At the beginning of Lent many Catholic parishes hand out little cardboard rice bowls to all of their members to encourage them to put money in the rice bowls at each meal during Lent. The people return the cardboard bowls to their parishes on Easter Sunday. Operation Rice Bowl gives seventy-five percent of the money to 1,200 international organizations to help people. Twenty-five percent of the money goes to local Catholic dioceses, so they can take away hunger in their very own neighborhoods and help people get back on their feet.

Some people raise money to buy them food...

Halfway across the nation in North Platte, Nebraska, teens walked to raise money for food banks. This amazing activity had youth walking three miles for a program called "Going Bananas Across America." The kids had their friends and relatives pledge money for every mile they walked. The profits from the walk went to twenty-one churches in different countries. The churches were in Haiti, in Tanzania, in Mexico, and in Peru. Some money also went to food banks in Nebraska.

Ben

...and some people experience hunger themselves.

In Portland, Oregon, teens wanted to know what it's like to be hungry, so they tried it for themselves. They fasted from food in order to feel more like people who don't have food to eat. Through fasting the students learned how much it hurts to be hungry. They learned that most hungry people around the world do not have a choice not to eat like they did.

World Youth Day

Feeding the souls of millions of Catholic teens across the globe, World Youth Day (WYD) is a huge gathering of young people that is hosted by the Pope. In 1986, Pope John Paul II held the first World Youth Day in Rome, Italy. Every other year since then, World Youth Day is held in Rome. The last one in Rome was in 2000. When WYD isn't in Rome, it is held somewhere else in the world. Some of the other places it has been held are Czestochowa, Poland (1991), Denver, Colorado (1993), Paris, France (1997) and Toronto, Canada (2002). The Pope started WYD to bring young people closer to God. (Pope means "Papa" in Latin, just in case you were wondering.)

Shannon Gunning, an eighteen-year-old from Littleton, Colorado, was touched by God when she attended the 2000 World Youth Day in Rome. Shannon told us that going to WYD inspired her. She was not involved in her community before attending, but at WYD Shannon felt a call from God to be more involved in her church. She says, "God sort of called me and I realized I couldn't sit back anymore." When

Shannon Gunning

she came back, she began helping out with Confirmation classes at her church.

Many people who come to World Youth Day are on a pilgrimage. A pilgrimage is a journey when people come together to make changes in their lives. Many times people will feel a change as the Holy Spirit fills their hearts. At WYD, people talk with each other, sing together and pray together. They do these things to get a closer connection with God and one another.

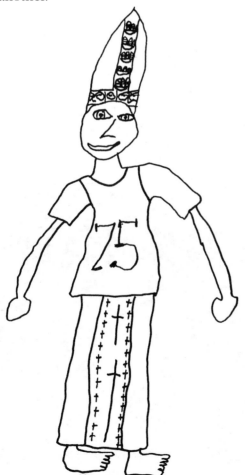

One of our authors who has been to Rome thinks that going to "World Youth Day would be like nothing you've ever seen before." He thinks this because he felt touched by the Holy Spirit when he received Holy Communion in the Vatican. The Holy Spirit just jumped down into his heart. We would encourage everyone who can to go to World Youth Day to learn more about God and themselves. Look up where the next World Youth Day is being held!

The Harlem Globetrotters have a new member on their team—Pope John Paul II! The Pope was made an honorary member and was given the number "75" because it was the team's 75th anniversary. They made him a member because he has done so much for the world and because he is really special to people all over. By doing good deeds and by being a kind leader, the Pope has helped many people get closer to God. The Harlem Globetrotters have shown their respect for our wonderful Pope.

Rachael Lampa

Rachael Lampa grew up with a lot of talent. Looking at her life, Rachael seems to be a regular girl from Boulder, Colorado, who plays basketball and talks like any other teenager. What does makes her different is that she is a fifteen-year-old singer who has already recorded a CD. As a little girl, Rachael could sing beautifully and now she uses her gift to feed people who are hungry for God.

in God's hands and God made her famous at the right time. If she would have become famous any earlier, she might not have been ready. However, Rachael's faith is more important to her than being famous. She hopes she can help people become closer to God, and she considers being able to sing for God a blessing.

Rachael encourages people not to be jealous of others' talents. She wants people to find the gifts that God has given them and use them to serve God.

Father Jerry Hogan

Have you ever been to a circus and seen a priest bless an elephant right in front of the

Rachael is a Catholic and Jesus is the center of her life. Rachael is very close to God and prays every day. Her faith is always growing and getting stronger. Rachael dedicated her CD to Jesus Christ. She called the album "Live For You." Rachael is proud of her CD and her favorite song on it is "Blessed."

Rachael has been on the *Tonight Show,* and she sang at World Youth Day for Pope John Paul. She put her talents

Beginning an illustration

In the circus, the flying acts are his favorite. He likes them because there is a lot of risk when the acrobat hanging from the swinging bar catches the person who has been soaring through the air. It reminds him of "being caught by God." Father Jerry also says, "The circus performers take their gifts from God and use them to relieve other people's pain."

Thomas Jones

Catholic astronaut Thomas Jones has visited space three times. His latest mission was to bring the U.S. laboratory module, Destiny, to the International Space Station. Mr. Jones can't believe the sight that he sees while flying out into space at 17,500 miles per hour. He loves the beauty of outer space and being able to

crowd? Father Jerry Hogan is a Catholic priest who travels around the U.S. with different circuses. He responds to people's hunger for God by hearing confessions, performing wedding ceremonies, celebrating Mass every day and showing the love and compassion of Jesus to those who are sick. Once, as a joke, he even asked a tiger if it wanted to go to confession.

look out the window and see the whole world before his eyes. Mr. Jones believes only God could have created the beauty he sees.

In space, Mr. Jones studies the readings for Mass just like Catholics on Earth do. He also has six Psalms given to him by a friend that he uses to pray with during free time. Mr. Jones puts his faith into action by feeding the hungry (himself) with spiritual food (the Bible and readings from daily Mass). He believes people should make time for Jesus and put their faith first, even in space.

John Michael Talbot

Imagine a man who was in a rock band and now sings music for God and feeds people spiritually. When John Michael Talbot was eighteen, he was performing with the rock group Mason Proffit. One night he was at a rock concert and all that he saw were beer bottles and drug jars shattered all over the floor. All of the sudden "living the life of a rock star seemed empty and sad to him." He did not want his life to be that way, so he left Mason Proffit and began to look for something more.

John Michael Talbot searched and looked into many religions. Then one day he saw an image of

John Michael Talbot

Photo credit: CNS photo by Nancy Wiechec

Jesus and began looking at different Christian communities. He decided to join the Catholic Church because he felt peace there.

One day he asked God what to do and God said, "Play your music and I will open and shut the doors for you." Now he plays his music for Jesus and sings to express his faith. John M. Talbot wants people to hear his music and get closer to Jesus.

"Lord, when did we see you thirsty and give you drink?" (Mt 25:37)

Adrian Flores

Adrian Flores lives in southern California. When he was young, he had never really been involved in the Church. He was involved in a lot of other activities but still felt like something was missing. One day his high school friends asked him to go on a retreat. Adrian didn't really want to go because he had been on a lot of retreats and he thought they were boring, but he decided to go anyway. When he got there, he was feeling really down. Adrian asked God to help him, and God did! At the end of the retreat, Adrian didn't want to leave and when he got home he couldn't wait to share what he had done. For the very first time, he told his family that he loved them.

While he was on the retreat, Adrian decided to join a group called the National Evangelization Team (NET). "National" stands for the teens that come from many parts of their country. "Evangelization" stands for bringing good news to others. "Team" stands for them being all together. The NET teams are like families. There are fifteen teams throughout the United States, Canada and Australia. The NET teams travel for nine months organizing retreats for kids who are middle and high school age. They go around in a van. Every member brings a suitcase, a backpack and his or her own sleeping bag. By their sacrifices, NET teams help young people satisfy their thirst for the Lord.

One time Adrian was at Saint Frances Cabrini parish in Lit-

Adrian Flores (in plaid shirt) with his NET team

tleton, Colorado. He was feeling kind of bad because the year was ending. A teenage boy came up and started talking to him. The young man had just become Catholic and thanked Adrian for sharing his faith. He gave Adrian a hug, told him he loved him and walked away. This was one of Adrian's favorite parts of the nine months.

Adrian said that if you want to do good work for God, praying is the most important thing you can do: "No matter where you are, God will always love you." He also said, "Give it all you've got. God will always be on your side." Adrian is a really good example of how faith is put into action.

Nick Alexander

Nick Alexander writes funny words to songs like, "I Got You Babe" by Sonny and Cher. His Catholic version of the song is called, "I Got You Saved."

Nick was born in Southern California but then moved to New York. Like his mother, Nick was an Episcopalian, but he was not very involved in his church. Nick's father was Catholic growing up, but he lost his faith and did not believe in God anymore. Growing up, Nick had the choice of going to church with his mother on Sundays or staying home with his father and doing chores. Sometimes he stayed home and sometimes he went to church.

Nick went to Rutgers University in New Jersey. He was in every Christian activity

on campus. One day Nick became interested in one particular activity and he was surprised to find out it was a Catholic group. While Nick was still in college, his mother bought him a book about Catholics and their faith. After Nick read the book, he prayed the rosary. He passed the book on to his friends and soon enough they were all praying the rosary together. Within the next two years they all became Catholic, including Nick.

After Nick became Catholic, he wrote good serious songs, and he also wrote some silly songs. Normally, Nick only played his serious songs in front of audiences, but they were not a big hit. One time he was asked to play his silly songs

Writing a book is hard work

and people laughed and laughed. They told him he should make a career singing his silly songs. So then Nick recorded a CD. When people thirst for joy and fun in their lives, Nick gives them his silly songs and makes them laugh. We are glad that he shares his musical talents and puts his faith into action by bringing joy to others.

Sister Rose Ann Fleming

Sister Rose has been a superintendent, a teacher and a college president. She has a law degree and a Ph.D. Now she is an academic advisor for Xavier University where she helps student athletes satisfy their thirst for a good education. Sister Rose will not give up on a kid even when it is very hard to help.

Sister Rose helps over 230 athletes keep up good grades so they can graduate. She makes sure they balance out their classes and helps them with their schedule. Sister Rose has helped 90% of the athletes graduate. In fact, 100% of the men's basketball players graduated.

Sister Rose reminds them to study and she makes sure they get their work in on time. If a student is out of town at a game, she will have his or her work faxed to her and she will get it to the teacher. Sister Rose says that anybody who can remember sports plays has a good mind for learning. This is Sister Rose's life. By helping the college kids make the grade, Sister Rose is putting her faith into action. Way to go, Sister Rose!

Christy Caruso

Have you ever heard of "Kids on Computers, Inc.?" While volunteering, a young woman noticed many children who

couldn't pay for computer education. Christy Caruso, a sixteen-year-old from Delray Beach, Florida, came up with an idea of collecting computers for kids who did not have the money to buy their own. So, with the help from her dad and uncle, she started her own company. Her family and friends help her to get donations and to repair the computers. She donates more than fifteen hours of her time every week to her business. Christy puts her faith into action by helping kids who need computers.

Regis Philbin

Regis Philbin is the host of *"Who Wants to be a Millionaire?"*, a popular TV show. He is a graduate of Notre Dame University. To show his thanks for his education, he gave the school 2.75 million dollars to build a 100-seat theatre. He saw a need and was there to help. Regis will get to go to the very first show for free. That was a generous way to put his faith into action!

"Lord, when did we see you a stranger and welcome you?" (Mt 25:38)

Mrs. Bernadette Henderson

"Writing a book is a noble deed," said Bernadette Henderson. This lady came from Australia to visit her friend in Denver, Colorado. When she heard about our book project, she decided to delay her trip and stay in Denver to help us...even though she didn't even know us! She welcomed us as her new friends, and she has added her special touch to the cooking projects in our book. Mrs. Henderson has put her faith into action by helping us with this book. We thank you very much, Mrs. Henderson, for sharing so much of your time with us this summer.

Tori Babin

Even though she's only sixteen years old, Tori Babin has been helping people all over the world. She traveled to Mexico to help build two different orphanages and she helped to baby-sit the children in them. She also helped to cook and clean. Then, Tori traveled to France where she helped to teach pre-school and visit the elderly.

Not only does Tori serve other countries, but she also puts her faith into action in her hometown of Denver, Colorado. She spends time working at the Samaritan House, working for clothing drives and soup kitchens, and helping children who have special needs. Tori enjoys her community service projects very much.

Tori believes there are "tons of opportunities. Anywhere you look there are plenty of people who need help." She said, "I think that putting your faith into action is a great way to serve God." Tori feels there is fun in doing service for others and helping people all over the world.

Tori Babin in action

Theresa McCullar

Theresa McCullar is happy to help

Theresa McCullar has done some very important acts of kindness for her family, friends and neighbors. She is eighteen years old and has been an active member in her youth group at her church. Theresa started going to her church youth group because her father had cancer and she needed some support. Through the youth group she got support for her problems and was reminded of her morals. Theresa said, "It's important to be in the youth group because it gives you a chance to talk about and share your faith."

Theresa became the president of the Key Club, a community service group, and encouraged other high school kids to volun-

teer. She has also worked for Camp Acoma. She said it was an "amazing experience." She has traveled to New Mexico to help out the people who live there. Theresa joined another program called People to People. This group traveled to Europe to learn about different cultures.

Volunteering makes Theresa feel happy and she says that it's fun to just forget about everything and help. "Life isn't so bad," she said. "God calls me every day to be kind." Theresa has inspired us to get up and do more for others.

Myriah L.

Jason Shin and Ben LaChance

Two young men from Denver, Colorado, really know how to put their faith

Jason Shin, Ben LaChance and friends repairing a fence

"Lord, when did we see you naked and clothe you?" (Mt 25:38)

David Billars

When David Billars got the idea to collect coats for homeless people who couldn't afford them, he told his Boy Scout troop about his idea. He and his troop started going door-to-door asking for coat donations. They traveled to churches and schools and David spoke at Mass telling people what he and his troop were doing. After all their hard work, they had 792 coats! They loaded the coats in a borrowed truck and zoomed downtown to the Samaritan House. At the Samaritan House David met the staff, the local news crew and a reporter for the *Denver Post*. They interviewed David. The next day, he was on the front page of the newspaper and on the TV evening news.

David is now twenty-two years old and is one of four children. When he was young he wanted to become an Eagle Scout, a dream that he made come

into action. Seventeen-year-old Jason Shin and fifteen-year-old Ben LaChance both worked with a Catholic Youth mission in San Rafael, New Mexico. They cleaned and fixed up a cemetery to show respect for the people buried there. Jason and Ben also helped clean a park by building a fence and pulling weeds.

Although the teens had to pay for their trip, they really enjoyed it. They spent three nights in the parish and the other three nights with different families. These two teens put their faith into action by making new friends and helping a town in need.

true! Something we forgot to say is David has Down Syndrome. But we want you to know he is just like anyone else. When we interviewed him it was just like we were speaking to any grown-up. David was really polite. He needed his mom to explain a few of our questions, but he always had answers for us.

David is a lot of fun to be around. He loves sports. When he was young, he played soccer. David also participated in the Special Olympics and got second place! Now he plays softball and basketball in a league.

David is a good reader and has an excellent sense of humor. He loves to play the

David Billars carrying a load of coats

drums. He graduated from high school in 1998. David works at a grocery store as a courtesy clerk. He puts groceries in bags and helps people bring the groceries to the car.

Just because someone has a disability, it doesn't mean they're not special. David is a very special person. People with disabilities are just like you and me on the inside and they deserve our respect. What we mean to say is, it doesn't matter if we're a little different on the outside. What really matters is what we're like on the *inside*.

Blanche St. Germaine and Sister Corona

Blanche St. Germaine crochets blankets for babies. Mrs. St. Germaine knows how to wrap a child in love because she has five of her own. She lives in Omaha, Nebraska, and works with Sister Corona, who also makes blankets for babies and women with unplanned pregnancies. Sister Corona hopes her kindness will help lower the number of abortions.

Because Mrs. St. Germaine raised her own kids in Maine, where it gets really cold, she knows how much babies need warm blankets. The two ladies share a job answering the phone and decided to work together making blankets too. Together they make at least one blanket a month, although it depends on how much the phone rings.

The ladies say they will make blankets as long as they have yarn. We think what they are doing is really nice. Mrs. St. Germaine prays for the babies as she makes the blankets. She thinks everyone should think about other people. We sure are glad that Sister Corona and Mrs. St. Germaine use their crocheting skills to put their faith in action.

project with two volunteers and six donated sewing machines. In six weeks, girls in fourth and fifth grades learned how to sew their own stuffed animals as well as fleece mittens. They donated the mittens to the Colorado Homeless Coalition. Some of the girls said they learned a lot, even how to sew on an old-fashioned sewing machine.

These girls do not just sell cookies and go on a few overnight field trips. They really love belonging to the Girl Scouts and enjoy helping the poor. These Girl Scouts have put their faith in action by sewing gifts for those in need.

"Lord, when did we see you ill and visit you?" (Mt 25:39)

Father Angelo D'Agostino

The spread of HIV and AIDS in America has been kept at a low rate because of good standards of living, quality health education and access to expensive medicine. But this isn't the case in places like Africa. The disease AIDS is far worse in Africa than in America. But one man is making a difference to help the children

Sew E-Z Program

Thirteen Catholic girls use their sewing skills to help others. They learned about sewing and charity through a program called Sew E-Z program in Denver, Colorado. The class was sponsored by the Mile High Council Girl Scouts' Outreach program. The program was run by their leader, Liz Shatlock, who went all the way through Girl Scouts and thinks this is a great way to give something back to their community. Liz started the service

Father Angelo D'Agostino

of Africa who are infected with the AIDS virus.

Father Angelo D'Agostino is from Providence, Rhode Island. He went through college in Vermont and became a medical doctor. This was only the beginning. He was drafted into the Air Force and served at a hospital in Washington, D.C. A few years later, he was ordained a Jesuit priest. After some time, his superiors asked him to study to become a psychiatrist. Later, he volunteered to serve as a missionary. His work called him to Thailand and then to Africa. In 1991, his eyes were opened to the serious problem of HIV and AIDS in young children living in Africa.

Father D'Agostino found out that kids in Africa who had HIV and AIDS were being abandoned on roadsides and in hospitals. The sad fact was that most of them were dying. Even if they were not dying, the kids were not accepted in their community, so they needed some place to live. Because of this, Father built an orphanage on two acres of land. Now there are seventy-six children living in ten houses. Father D'Agostino considers this a small village. He decided to name the new program "Nyumbani," which means "hospice" in Swahili.

Father D'Agostino has made sure that his orphans are very well cared for by giving them regular medical treatment and sending them to school. Hundreds of babies, children and teens have been helped by Nyumbani.

Father D'Agostino said he took on this enormous task because all children are children of God. They deserve care. He feels that he is an instrument of God who can show compassion. At the age of seventy, Father D'Agostino has found this to be his most rewarding work yet. As you can see through Father D'Agostino's example, one single person can make a big difference in the lives of others. After all, the Bible did say, "When did you see me ill and visit me?" Father and all the others working with Nyumbani have put their faith into action.

Write and rewrite!

Kevin

Seton House

In downtown Denver, Colorado, there is a small house hiding behind the huge towering buildings, but its light is bright. The Seton House draws men with AIDS to its light to be helped. This house gives

Kaitlyn T.

men a place to come and live. The Seton House is very beautiful. Outside, behind a gate, there is a statue of Jesus and just beyond is a statue of Mary on a fountain.

The Seton House is a special place where the Sisters of the Missionaries of

Charity, founded by Mother Teresa, take care of men with AIDS who are dying. Up to fifteen men can live in the building. Many of the men said they had some-

Sisters, residents and volunteers at Seton House

thing missing from their lives for a long time. God was missing from their lives. At the Seton House their faith has been restored.

Also living at the Seton House are Mother Teresa's nuns who run the place. Something special about the sisters is that they rely on the goodness of strangers to provide what they need. The nuns go to church every morning so they may ask for God's help. They gave up everything they owned to go and live with God. The sisters put their faith in action by feeding the men and taking care of them spiritually.

With the help from volunteers, the sisters prepare delicious meals. For breakfast the volunteers make things like bacon, eggs, hash browns and toast. Then the volunteers continue their service by washing dishes after the residents are finished eating.

The men at the Seton House follow the nuns' examples of loving one another and putting their faith in action. They help one another with their problems in life by praying with each other. Some of the men realize they do not need all of their material possessions and even donate some things to other people. As one of the residents of the Seton House commented, "Stay with God through all the good and bad times. He is always with you!"

Locks of Love

Catholic Youth Organization (CYO) members from Saint Peter Catholic Church in New Orleans, Louisiana, help the Locks of Love organization during Lent. (The word "lock" used in this way means a piece of hair.) The Locks of Love program helps kids from seven years old

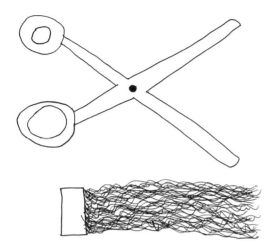

donations came from family members of people that have died of cancer or who have cancer themselves. Even though some members of the CYO group don't grow long enough hair to be donated, they help in other ways, like by washing the hair that has been donated. Many people, along with CYO members from Saint Peter's Church, have helped kids with cancer live a better life.

"Lord, when did we see you in prison and visit you?" (Mt 25:39)

Christian Molidor

Christian Molidor is an average person from Denver, Colorado. He likes to spend time with his wife and son and enjoys sports and reading. But he stands apart from the crowd, because he also enjoys helping people. Mr. Molidor believes that people should be kind to one another, as well as patient and forgiving. The people he likes to help are people who are in prison.

to seventeen years old who have cancer and have lost their hair because of medical treatments. People with long hair donate their hair to make wigs for children with cancer. They say it is a sacrifice to cut their hair, but they don't mind because their hair will grow back again. They know they are doing a good deed by helping kids.

Normally it takes about twelve pony tails to make a single wig. A store-bought wig made from real hair would be very, very expensive. Kids with cancer who are involved in the Locks of Love program do not have to pay any money for the wigs that are given to them. The CYO members who donate their hair really care about the kids with cancer even though they don't know them.

Most people who donate are women, because they have long hair. Also, many

Christian Molidor

Mr. Molidor spreads the word of God to prisoners, mostly young ones. He sits down to talk to them and he helps them find ways to solve their problems. He tries to help them make good choices and turn their lives in the right direction.

When someone gets involved with gangs, they need someone to dig them out. Sometimes their parents aren't there to do it. For a young girl named Rose, things were looking pretty bad. But Mr. Molidor came to see her and helped her dig herself out of her hole. When she got out of jail, Rose started working with and helping kids in gangs, too.

By using the talent God blessed him with and by putting his faith into action, Mr. Molidor helps young people with troubles turn their lives over to God. His belief and hope is that if people start working with each other nicely, maybe they will keep people from coming back to jail.

Youth authors in a thoughtful moment

The McCabes

Josette and Michael McCabe are a couple who also visit inmates in prison in Colorado. The inmates at the prison appreciate the visits because it lets them know that someone cares about them. By visiting with the prisoners, Josette and Michael help them to become closer to God. In fact, three people have be-

come Christians and two have been baptized Catholic! The McCabes said, "Our lives have changed because we know we are helping."

Patrick Atkinson

In the streets of New York, Patrick Atkinson was working with young people who ran away or who were addicted to drugs. After another troubled teenager died, Mr. Atkinson decided he couldn't take it anymore and he asked for a change in work. When he was told to go to Guatemala to work, he was shocked. But knowing this was what God wanted, he packed up and left.

Mr. Atkinson, who is from North Dakota, arrived in Guatemala in 1983. His Spanish vocabulary didn't go far past "hola" which means hello and "burrito," but he knew that he could learn Spanish. Due to a civil war in Guatemala, working there was very dangerous. Sometimes people even shot at him. Once a bomb exploded outside his hotel and knocked him out of bed. Mr. Atkinson didn't leave Guatemala, though, because he knew that working with the Guatamalan people is what God wanted him to do.

With God's help, he started a program called "The God's Child Project." Schools and parishes send money and supplies from North America to help feed, clothe, and educate over 2,500 children who are poor. By helping the children learn, Mr. Atkinson helps free them from the prison of poverty that comes from no education. He teaches them that they can do anything they set their minds to.

The God's Child Project has also helped many adults. Some of those adults are in prison. People from the project help the prisoners by visiting them, by feeding them, and by repairing the prison building.

Mr. Atkinson said, "God clearly loves his children very much and doesn't want them living on the streets." So he continues working with people who are poor or in prison. When Mr. Atkinson gets tired and wants to quit, the Catholic Church is like a "floaty" holding him up until he can swim alone again.

The civil war in Guatemala officially ended in 1996, but Mr. Atkinson continues his ministry with children. We think he is a very brave man for putting God's people first in his life.

Cardinal Anthony Bevilacqua

In Philadelphia, Pennsylvania, Cardinal Anthony Bevilacqua is an inspiration for the inmates in prisons. He reminds them that they are always welcome in the Church. He tells them, "The Church loves you very much, because Christ loves you very much." He also tells them, "No matter what you've done, you can always become a saint—always." His big message is

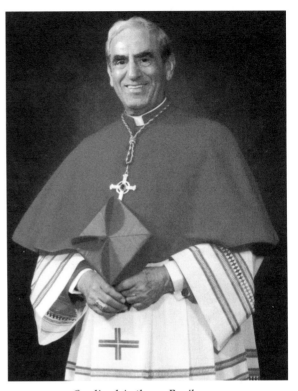

Cardinal Anthony Bevilacqua

that God wants to forgive everyone for their sins. He always tells prisoners that God is merciful. He talks many prisoners through what they have done until they are truly sorry and can be forgiven by God. Wow!

"Amen, I say to you, whatever you did for the least of my brothers, you did for me" (Mt 25:40).

All of the people in our chapter have spent their time helping others and helping Jesus. We are very thankful for them and for the things they have done. Just like the people in this chapter, God has given all of us talents. As God tells us in the Bible, he wants us to give our gifts back to him by using them to help each other.

You have talents that you can use, too. We want to help you find your talents and come up with ways to use them. You may want to talk to people at your church or talk to people in your community.

Before you can use your talents, you have to know what they are. Use the lines below to help you.

I am good at:

_____

_____

_____

_____

I am interested in:

_____

_____

_____

_____

Now, say a prayer and thank God for the gifts and talents he has given you. Next, ask God how he wants you to use your talents. Write down the ideas he gives you:

_____

_____

_____

_____

These ideas you have written are the things you can do or the places you can go. Now…go and serve! God bless you as you put your faith into action!

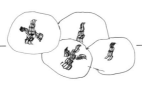

HANDS-ON FUN

Do you like cooking or things in art?
Are you looking for something fun from the start?
Then "Hands-on Fun" is right for you!
We're sure you'll enjoy everything that we do!

Do you like to make or bake things? We bet you didn't know that learning about our Catholic faith can involve arts and crafts and cooking! Well, it can. If you like both God and art, Hands-on Fun is just for you. Learn how to make things like rosaries and special Good Deed Beads. Bake things like pretzels and delicious Resurrection Buns. Have fun!

CRAFTS

Advent Wreaths

What is green, round, has three purple candles and one pink candle, and helps us get ready for Jesus' coming? An Advent wreath!

Advent is a get-ready-for-Christmas time. It starts four weeks before Christmas. During this time many families use Advent wreaths to help them prepare their hearts for Jesus' birthday.

The tradition of praying around the Advent wreath comes from the people of Germany. The wreath's green color stands for eternal life. The circular shape represents the unending love of Christ. There are four candles on the Advent wreath. The first purple candle tells us to prepare for Jesus' coming. The second purple candle is our hope that he is going to come again soon. The third candle (pink) is to rejoice. It is exciting! The fourth purple candle shows our love for Christ. On Christmas Day, you put a white

Advent wreath

candle in the middle and light it. This candle stands for Jesus. We call it the Christ Candle. The flame represents the light of Christ coming into our families' lives. That is what Advent is all about.

You can make an Advent wreath in different ways using many materials. It just has to be green, circular, and have three purple candles and one pink candle. You should decorate it respectfully.

We made our Advent wreath out of clay and green glitter. To make the clay you need 1 cup of water, 1 cup of corn starch and 1 cup of salt. Add green food coloring to get a nice Christmas green color. Mix all of the above things in a bowl until the clay gets smooth. Shape it into a bagel or donut shape but bigger, like a plate. Use a candle to press four holes for the candles. Let it dry. Now decorate it!

We don't really know about the history of the Advent wreath, but we think it could have begun like this:

Perhaps a long time ago in Germany, there lived a little girl and boy. They

Preparing clay for the Advent wreath

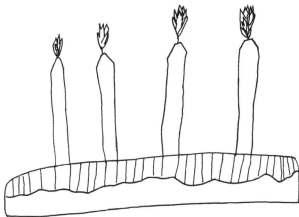

loved Jesus with all their hearts, minds and souls. Not everyone else in the town believed in Jesus. The two children thought they should do something about this. They thought and thought until it was five weeks before Christmas. Then the girl said, "We should make something that means Jesus is coming." So they both went to Mass, and after Mass they asked the priest what word meant the same as coming. The priest said that Advent meant the same as coming. The children said thanks and went home. Then they decided that they would make an Advent wreath. So they went outside and found some pine branches and put them in a circle. They asked the candle makers if they had four extra candles. The candlemakers gave the kids three purple candles and one pink candle. The children stuck them in the wreath and they told everyone about the wreath and how it could be used to prepare people for Jesus'

second coming and how it could remind them of Jesus' birth. The children felt great!

You can learn more about Advent wreaths, like why purple and pink candles are used and when to light them, by reading a book or talking to a priest. Have fun!

Rosaries

Did you know that the rosary is a powerful prayer that can sometimes lead to miracles? For example, when our friend Shannon's mom prayed for healing because she had a brain tumor and was pregnant, the rosary helped her. The prayers gave her the strength to go through the surgery and have a healthy baby.

Rosaries have been used for prayer for a long time. In the early 13th century,

Learning the rosary knots

Mary appeared to Saint Dominic and she gave him a rosary. Mary told Saint Dominic how to pray the rosary and said that anyone who prayed it would have grace. She said, "This is the precious gift which I leave to you." Saint Dominic went a-round teaching people how to use the rosary. Pretty soon, over 100,000 people were praying the rosary!

Hard at work on rosaries

To make a rosary you will need:

- One six-foot length of cord
- 53 beads of one color to use for the Hail Mary prayers
- 6 beads of a different color to use for the Our Father prayers
- 1 rosary knot-making tool (optional)

Directions:

1. Tie a knot two inches from one end of the string.

2. Put 10 beads on the string.

3. Tie a strong knot.

4. Put an Our Father bead on.

5. Tie another strong knot. That was your first decade.

6. String ten more beads for your second decade.

7. Tie a knot again.

8. Add an Our Father bead and tie another knot.

9. Repeat the steps 5 through 7 for the next two decades.

Young author records the rosary making process

10. For the last decade string on ten beads, then tie a knot.

11. DO NOT add another Our Father bead!

12. Take both ends and tie them in a big knot. Cut off the shorter string close to the knot.

13. Take the longer string, and put on an Our Father bead.

14. Tie a knot. Now string on three beads for the Hail Marys.

15. Tie another knot. Add one Our Father bead.

16. Pull the string through the crucifix. Tie a knot.

17. Cut off the tails of the longer string, and put clear fingernail polish on the knots where you cut off the ends of the strings. You have now completed a rosary!

(You can also get rosary making kits that come with their own special directions.)

We make rosaries because we think it's fun to help out all the people who are poor and don't have one. We feel that God likes it when we make rosaries. Sometimes we make six in one month. We give them to a missionary and he takes them to different places. Mary promised many graces to those who pray the rosary regularly. Many families pray the rosary together. If you'd like to learn how to pray the rosary, there are many books available. We feel good when we pray the rosary because we can get closer to God and heaven. So can YOU!

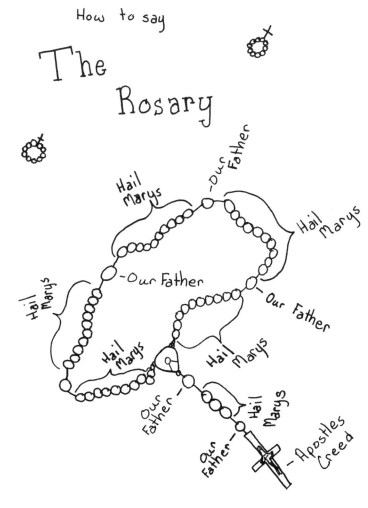

How to say

The Rosary

Good Deed Beads

Do a good deed,
Move a bead.
Feed the poor,
Move one more.
Give your friends the help they need,
You can add another bead.
Help clean up the kitchen floor.
Guess what? Now that's four!

In the 1800s Thérèse Martin's older sister gave her something called Good Deed Beads. She said these were some beads that could help you count your presents to God. One day Thérèse was picking flowers and it was her grandmother's turn to bring flowers to church for the altar. Thérèse didn't want to give the flowers she picked to her grandmother. Then Thérèse remembered the Good Deed Beads and she gave the flowers to her grandmother. Thérèse Martin grew up and became a nun. Today, we know her as Saint Thérèse of Lisieux, so we guess the Good Deed Beads made her think of God more.

The Good Deed Beads have a crucifix on the bottom and a religious medal on top. In the middle are ten beads. Every time you do a good deed, you pull a bead towards the crucifix.

To make your own beads you will need these things: a piece of string 18 inches long, ten wooden or pony beads, a crucifix and a religious medal of your choice. First, take the medal and put it in the middle of the string. Tie a knot right after you put the medal on. Take a bead and put the string through one of the beads from one side. Then take the other end of the string and put it through the opposite side of the bead, and then pull both the strings tight. Do that until you have ten beads strung. When you are finished with the tenth bead, leave a space about an inch long and tie on a crucifix. You can pull the beads up or down. This allows you to move one bead at a time. Pull a bead closer to the crucifix when you do a good deed.

You can make one for everyone in the family, and at the end of the day tell God how many beads you and your family pulled. Keep it in your pocket as a reminder to do good deeds, to think of Jesus and to pray to God. This project was so fun and exciting! Good Deed Beads

are a great way to know that you have done good things.

Holy Water Bottles

Holy water is blessed by a priest on Holy Saturday or when needed. That is

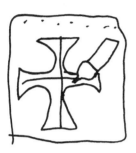

what makes it special. Holy water is used for baptism. It cleans and purifies you. What people do with holy water most often is they put it on two fingers and make the sign of the cross on themselves when they enter and leave church. This reminds people that they are baptized Catholics.

Holy water is important to Catholics because the devil hates things that are blessed with holy water. It will help you when the devil tries to tempt you.

Most families don't have holy water in their homes. We decorated these great bottles so we could take holy water to our homes. We made them as wonderful as we could because they were for God's holy water. Now we have a container to carry our holy water from church to our homes. You will need a container to carry your holy water from church to your home also.

Here is how you can make one. Choose a container or a jar with a lid. It can be any size depending on how you want to use it. A tiny one will fit in your pocket. A large jar would be good if you want a lot of holy water at home.

WARNING: if you try this project, the paint can be hard to control! Take your jar and lid and decorate with fabric paint, buttons, stickers, spray paint, enamel or fabric. Some symbols you can use to decorate your bottle are angels, doves, peace signs, shamrocks (a symbol of the Trinity), crosses, candles, or fish. Let the paint dry for a few hours. Then take the jar to church and get

Decorating holy water bottles

some holy water. Now you have your very own holy water container.

If for some reason you no longer want the holy water, pour it out onto the ground or bury it so it will go back to nature. Don't pour it into a sink because it will go into the sewer and that is no place for holy water.

These holy water jars are wonderful things to have. We all think you should try this at home. Have fun doing this exciting project.

The Ribbon Cross

The cross is a symbol of the death and resurrection of Jesus. A cross reminds us that we are Christian. When we think of the cross, we think of Jesus. We think the cross is a happy sign because HE loves us so much that he died for us so that we could be saved. We lost our Lord on the cross. It was a horrible loss, but in three days, the Lord rose. Each post of the cross that juts out from the middle of the cross points to different parts of the world, but they all begin with Jesus, who is the center of our world.

There are very many different kinds of crosses. The cross we made was the ribbon cross. This is how you make it:

Supplies:

- One six-foot length of cord
- 1 plastic cross-stitch canvas (about 3" by 3")
- 1-3/4 yards of 1/8 inch ribbon
- 3 stacking beads

Directions:

Draw a cross like the diagram with a washable marker on cross-stitch canvas

Making ribbon crosses

Hands-on fun!
Ribbon Cross

Cross pattern:

X = Hold end of ribbon behind here

The cross:

diagonally. Continue to follow our diagram and go down diagonally.

When you have done this enough times to cover go back through a hole near the center then go across. Go diagonally in the center to secure the ribbon. Then run it through the top hole. Tie beads on the ends of your ribbons and double knot them neatly.

The ribbon cross can then be used for a bookmark, a decoration or to give to a friend. You could even put it in your pocket to remind you that Jesus is always with you.

RECIPES

Lenten Hot Cross Buns

A long time ago, a monk in England was baking buns from a special recipe his mother gave to him. Easter was coming and he felt sorry for the poor people on the streets that had no food. The man baked extra buns and added raisins and spices. Because it was Lent, he decorated them with a white frosting cross. The baker then gave out the buns to the poor. One boy was so proud that he would not eat

and cut it out. Weave the ribbon through the canvas starting in the center. Leave some ribbon, in the center, about the size of your pinkie. Then go up to the center top hole and put the ribbon through it. Then go directly to the center bottom hole and pull the ribbon through. Go up the buns. Instead, he said he would rather sell them than eat them. He went through the streets singing this tune:

Hot Cross Buns, Hot Cross Buns.

One a penny, two a penny, Hot Cross Buns.

If you haven't got a daughter, give one to your son.

One a penny, two a penny, Hot Cross Buns.

After the boy sold all of the buns, he gave the money to the church. What he did was a very big sacrifice. Today Hot Cross Buns are still a favorite tradition on Good Friday in many places. Christians have chosen the buns and the cross as a symbol of the resurrection and new life

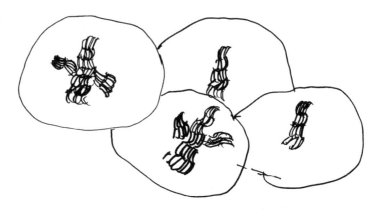

of Jesus. To make your own Hot Cross Buns, you will need these ingredients:

- 1 tsp. cinnamon
- 1/2 tsp. ginger
- 1/2 tsp. allspice
- 2 tbs. grated orange peel
- Five raisins each bun
- One package of frozen bread dough (thawed)

Directions:

Mix the cinnamon, ginger, allspice, and grated orange peel in a bowl.

Take one slice of dough per person from the package. Flatten the dough slices with the palm of your hand.

Fold spices and raisins into the dough and pinch together on the top.

Bake at 400°F for 8–10 minutes. When the buns are finished and cooled, put a white cross on the top of each one with frosting.

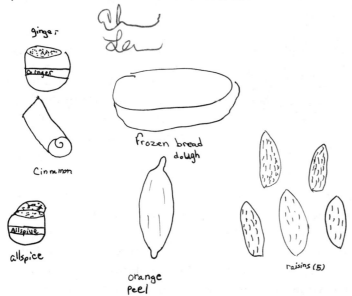

EASTER COOKING PROJECTS

Resurrection Buns

This is a song we wrote to the tune of "Are You Sleeping?" to sing while you are making Resurrection Buns:

> *Resurrection, resurrection.*
> *Wake up now, wake up now.*
> *Everybody come and look.*
> *Everybody come and look.*
> *He is gone! He is gone!*

Here is the story behind the Resurrection Buns:

The women were very sad because their best friend had died three days before. They were walking toward the tomb where their best friend lay. Their best friend's name was Jesus. When they got to the tomb, the women were suprised that the stone had been rolled away. They gasped! All of a sudden, a man dressed in white appeared. He was shining like the sun. "Don't be afraid," he told them. "Jesus has been raised up. Go and tell his friends." Then the women ran and told the disciples what had happened.

We did a neat project. The project was about the resurrection of Jesus. Just as the soldiers and the followers of Jesus were surprised to find the tomb empty, you will find a big surprise when you do our project.

Ingredients:

- Canned refrigerated biscuits (for the tomb)
- Large marshmallows (for Jesus)

marshmallow

bread dough

Directions:

Open the canned biscuit dough. Pretend that the marshmallow is the

Flattening out the dough

Making Easter cookies

Easter Cookies

Easter cookies, made out of ordinary cookies, are fun and easy to make. They are crispy and crunchy. When you make them it's like a mystery, because you don't know exactly what will happen next. Everything you use to make these cookies has a symbol. You make them in the order of Jesus' crucifixion and resurrection.

The cookies look so good you just want to eat them all, but of course if you did that, you would get a stomach-ache. These cookies are wonderful for any age. These "sweet tooth" quenchers are sure to bring smiles to the faces of all who eat them.

They are called Easter Cookies because once you get them out of the oven there is a mystery you have to solve which reminds Christians of Easter!

Ingredients:

- 1 cup whole pecans
- zipper baggie
- 1 tsp. vinegar
- wooden spoon
- 3 egg whites
- mixing bowl
- pinch salt
- waxed paper
- cookie sheet
- tape
- Bible

body of Jesus. Put the body of Jesus marshmallow on some flattened out dough. Fold the dough over the marshmallow; pinch the dough tightly on the top to seal the marshmallow in (kind of like when they sealed Jesus in the tomb). Make sure none of the marshmallow is showing.

Place the buns on a large greased baking pan and put it in the oven. Bake in the oven at 350°F and set the timer for 10–12 minutes. Take out of the oven and let cool. Take a bite and look for a surprise inside.

These Resurrection Buns are a great project to share with a friend. You are not only in for a great surprise, but you will be able to share a wonderful reminder of Jesus' resurrection together. Enjoy!

Here are the directions:

Preheat the oven to 300°F.

1. Put all the pecans in the zipper baggie and let everyone beat them with the wooden spoon to break them into pieces. Tell everyone that after Jesus was arrested the Roman soldiers beat him. Read: John 19:1-3.

2. Let everyone smell the vinegar and if someone wants to taste it, let them taste what Jesus tasted. Put one teaspoon of vinegar into the bowl. Tell them that when Jesus was on the cross and thirsty, he was given vinegar to drink. Read: John 19:28-30.

3. Add the egg whites to the vinegar. Beat the egg whites and vinegar until soft peaks form. The symbol of egg whites stands for life. To give us life, Jesus gave up his life. Read: John 10:10-11.

4. Add a pinch of salt in the bowl. Sprinkle a tiny bit of salt into your hand and taste it. The salt represents the tears of people crying for Jesus. It also represents the bitterness of our sins. Read: Luke 23:27.

5. At first the ingredients won't taste very good. Then we added a cup of sugar, which was a symbol of Jesus' sweetness. Add the sugar a little at a time and keep beating. Jesus died on the cross because he loved us and he wanted to show us that he wanted to forgive our sins. Read: Psalm 34:8 and John 3:16.

6. Beat the egg whites and sugar about 12-15 minutes until stiff peaks are made. God is pure like the egg whites and sugar. Read: Isaiah 1:18 and John 3:1-3.

7. Gently stir the nuts into the egg whites in the bowl. Put cookie dough on wax paper on a baking sheet. Tell others that each cookie is a symbol of Jesus' rocky tomb. Read: Matthew 27:57-60.

8. Put the baking sheet in the oven and turn the oven off. Use pieces of masking tape to seal the oven. This is just like Jesus' tomb. Read: Matthew 27:65-66.

9. GO TO BED! You might feel sad to have to go to bed instead of eating the cookies, but remember how Jesus' followers and disciples were VERY sad when Jesus' tomb was sealed. Read: John 16:20 and 22.

10. When you wake up on Easter, "unseal" the oven and give everyone a cookie. The cookie will have a cracked surface like the tomb. When you take a bite, the cookie will be hollow! Jesus' followers were shocked to find no one in the tomb, and to find the tomb open on the first Easter! Once they found that Jesus had risen they felt very excited and happy and so should you! Read: Matthew 28:1–9. HE HAS RISEN!

MORE COOKIES

We would like to tell you about three types of cookies that are symbols of our faith. They are the shamrock, candy cane and the stained glass cookies. All you need is your favorite sugar cookie dough and some time to create fun! Roll out and bake the cookies as directed in your recipe.

Shamrock Cookies

A shamrock symbolizes the Holy Trinity. Saint Patrick used a shamrock to teach the people about the Holy Trinity. He picked a shamrock and, pointing to its three sections, said, "The Father, Son, and Holy Spirit!"

You might want to use some green food coloring to add color to the dough. Use a floured cookie cutter to cut out a shamrock. Decorate the cookie using green sprinkles. Bake as directed and taste! You can tell when you take a bite that you are learning about your faith because there are three parts to eat!

Candy Cane Cookies

Did you know that way back in the 1600s mothers used sugar sticks for pacifiers? Later on, at Christmastime, someone made the sticks in the shape of a shepherd's staff or a cane. Moms used these little candy canes to occupy  their small children during the Christmas services. It was during the 1800s, that the candy cane was brought to the United States by a half-German, half-Swedish immigrant who came to Wooster, Ohio.

The candy cane can represent an upside down "J" for Jesus or a shepherd's staff. The red represents the blood Jesus shed for us and the white represents the pureness of Jesus. This is another symbol used to share our Catholic faith with others.

Just take some sugar cookie dough and divide it into two bowls. Use red food coloring to make one ball of red dough. Leave the other plain. Make two balls of dough (about the size of a walnut). Roll the red between your hands into a long snake. Next roll the white. Twist the two tubes together and form into the shape of a candy cane. Bake as directed in the recipe. Enjoy the candy cane cookie reminders of Jesus!

Cutting out stained glass cookies

Stained Glass Cookies

A long time ago, when a lot of people didn't know how to read, churches used brightly colored stained glass windows to tell the stories of our religion. Stained glass cookies are cookies that look like they have stained glass inside. They really have melted, crushed-up lifesavers in them. In some ways stained glass cookies are like us. When the sun shines through stained glass in churches it gives off bright colors. When Jesus' light shines through us we give off kindness and a bright smile. You can create these tasty cookies as reminders of God's love.

First separate the lifesavers by color and put each set in a zipper baggie. Put a

Audrey Verlovec

towel over the bag and crush the lifesavers with a rolling pin or small hammer. Take some sugar cookie dough and roll it out. Use cookie cutters to make shapes. Then use a smaller cookie cutter or a safe knife to cut a shape out of the inside. Put the cookie on parchment paper on a cookie sheet. Fill the hole with the crushed lifesavers. Bake as directed.

After the cookies have baked and cooled, be sure to hold one up to the light to see the "stained glass." The next time you make cookies, think about making these to remind you to let "your light shine" for Jesus.

THE STORY OF THE PRETZEL

Pretzels are a symbol that have been around since the fifth century. People believe that a monk twisted bread dough in the shape of a heart, with a twist in the middle to remind people to pray during the Lenten season. This may have come from praying by crossing your arms and placing your hands on your shoulders. Pretzel means "little arms." Here are some interesting stories for your enjoyment. Happy reading!

Once there were three children. Every day they would walk past the bakery. They would stand by it and take in deep breaths of the beautifully scented air. One day, Ash Wednesday to be exact, the bakery smelled especially good. Soon the baker came out and gave each child a twisted piece of bread. He said, "These are pretzels. Every time you see a pretzel say: 'Dear Jesus, I love you. Dear Jesus, I adore you. Dear Jesus, stay in my heart forever.'"

The children repeated this. "This is good," said the baker. "Now take these pretzels to three people and tell them what I told you." They did as he said and went home. The next day they were standing outside the bakery sniffing the air when the baker came out. "We did what you told us to do," said the children. "I see," replied the baker, and then he gave the children more pretzels. "Give these pretzels to more people and then go and eat the others," he said. The children did just that, and by Easter the children had given out so many pretzels that everyone in the town knew about the

Preparing the pretzel dough

pretzels and were saying the pretzel prayer. Can you remember to say this prayer whenever you see a pretzel?

The first pretzel in the United States was brought here by a beggar. The beggar smelled a delightful aroma as he passed by the bakery of Julius Sturges. The beggar asked the baker for some food, and the baker gave him a whole meal. In return, the beggar gave the baker the recipe for soft pretzels. One of the workers decided to try making this new kind of bread. The workers loved it! In a very short time many people were requesting soft pretzels from the bakery. The Julius Sturges Pretzel House is still in business in Lititz, Pennsylvania.

We heard this story about hard pretzels too. The first hard pretzels were made by accident. The pretzels were cooking over the fire, when the apprentice cook fell asleep. The fire went out, and the worker woke up. He thought the pretzels had never been baked, so he put the pretzels back into the fire. His boss was furious! Soon however, he was munching. Everyone really liked this new taste. Then those pretzels caught on.

These stories of the pretzel have become connected to our Christian background because of the shape of the pretzel and the way it reminds us of pray-

ing. The pretzel will always have a place in our hearts.

Soft Pretzel Recipe:

- 1 package active dry yeast
- 1/2 cup of lukewarm water
- 1 tsp. of sugar
- 4 cups of flour
- egg, beaten
- Coarse salt or any other topping you may choose

Directions:

Dissolve yeast in the water. Add salt, sugar and flour. Knead for 5–10 minutes, adding more flour as needed to reduce stickiness. Twist the dough into shapes. Place on Teflon baking sheet, brush with beaten egg, sprinkle with topping and bake at 425°F for 15 minutes or until lightly brown.

Decorated Sweet Cross

SWEET CROSSES

Do you want to make a really wonderful dessert for a very special occasion like Easter, a First Communion, or a Confirmation party that everyone will love? We found the best special dessert ever, Sweet Crosses!

We think this was the best thing we made in cooking because it was sweet, satisfying, pretty and easy to make. As soon as you taste this sweet cake, a happy smile will light up your face. It was so good that my dad ate mine before I could have one bite!

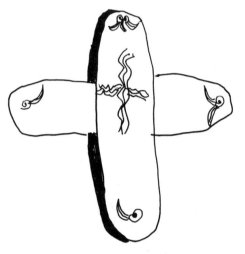

You will love this sweet, sweet cross. The shape of the Twinkies put together looks like a cross. The cross represents Jesus' death and resurrection. And here's how we made these crosses:

Make your favorite frosting. Divide it into parts and add coloring. Besides the frosting you will need 2 Twinkies for each cross, 3 icing bags, or tubes of frosting filled with different colored frosting, to make icing flowers, and a knife.

To make Sweet Crosses, leave one Twinkie whole. This will be the one that goes across. Then take the other Twinkie and cut 1/3 off of the top. This will be the top part of the cross. The remaining piece will be the bottom of the cross. Use a little icing to attach the horizontal bar to the vertical pieces. Frost the top surface of the cross. Use icing bags filled with colored icing to make five flower decorations and leaves on the cross. These flowers remind us of the five wounds of Jesus. We loved these Sweet Crosses, and we think you will, too!

We hope you enjoyed learning about the wonderful things we did during our writing workshop. At our local library we found several books that had tons of things to do in them. You may want to look for them. We want you to know that there are many things that help us learn about our faith and think of God. They are fun to do and teach us to be better people too.

Shannon
Frisbie

OUR VISION FOR A BETTER TOMORROW

We have enjoyed learning about our Catholic faith. One of the most important things we found out is that our Catholic faith can help us on our journey through life to heaven. Our Church helps us grow in faith and challenges us to love Jesus Christ and share his Gospel.

Here are some things that we learned during our writing workshop:

Young authors jotting down their dreams and hopes

We learned that…

We are proud to be Catholic Christians.

Miracles do happen. In fact, we think this book is one of them.

Faith is more than listening; it is *doing*.

You need to let God help you through life.

God is our loving Father.

We are all links in a chain. If we help someone up when they fall, it might inspire others to help someone else.

God works in so many different ways.

Even one person can make a difference.

We don't have to wait until we grow up to be authors.

We should do our best in everything we do.

Here is our vision for a better tomorrow:

We hope that...

People will better understand our Catholic faith.

By learning about how people put their faith into action, others will be inspired to do the same thing.

Everyone will learn to be kind to one another, no matter what the differences between them are.

More people will pray and use all that God gives us in the Church.

All Catholics and others will show respect for all religions and cultures.

We also have some special prayers for YOU:

We pray that ...

All of us will become saints because God calls us to be holy people.

You will listen to the call that God gives you and let him guide you to your vocation.

You will put your faith into action to make the world a better place.

By reading this book, you will learn more about the Catholic faith and grow closer to God.

For all of these intentions, we pray to the Lord. Lord, hear our prayer!

YOUNG WRITERS WORKSHOP PARTICIPANTS

Judith H. Cozzens, Director

Student Authors

Lia N. Alexander
Kateri E. Aubrecht
Selina Banuelos
Shannon Marie Baylie
Jennifer B. Bissel
Paul J. Bruin
Christina M. Buches
Katelian Buljung
Matt J. Burch
Max Bush
Anna Carpinello
Megan C. Casey
Courtney L. Cochran
Linzy R. Coffey
Maeve Cohen
Caitlin Nichole Connelly
Carolyn Ann Crabtree

Kay M. Dea
Richard Deanda
Heidi E. Deisch
Patrick C. DiMarco
Christina Dones
Rachel Elizabeth Donnelly
Jacque Fankell
Judy Farrow
Kevin A. Farrow
Kristofer J. Ferree
Stefan T. Fletcher
Shannon Lea Frisbie
Samantha M. Fromme
Michael Gallegos
Kristeena M. Gallegos
Victor U. Galvan Ramirez
Ruby A. Gonzalez
Sarah Guese
Michelle Nicole Hanna
Katelin Healy Hazelwood
Ryan M. Heath
Alexander Hendricks
Cecilia Holm

Colleen Ann Hopkins
Juliann K. Hopkins
C. J. Hopkins
Catherine E. Jensen
Hallie L. Kaiser
Adam Carl Kaufman
James R. Kealohi
Sarah E. Kelly
Myriah Lynn LaChance
Jordana L. LaChance
Hannahh LaChance
Baylen A. Lessner
Elizabeth Marie Levario
John J. Lilles
Nate Lotze

Matthew Christian Love
Erin F. Lowrey
Andrew T. Lowrey
Sarah Marie Lyons
Alexander Ross MacNabb
Nhu Mai
Benjamin McCabe
Joshua James McCabe
Evan Russel McCombs
Analisa Meyer

Erik A. Mida
Jake Montgomery
Alexandra Moore
Joseph B. Moran
Luke A. Moscoso
Taylor Naughton
Danai Noftz
Aleigha Ann Perez
Kyle Price
Nicholas Michael Prudhomme

Jillian Michelle Quintana
Melissa A. Ripper
Kevin T. Ripper
Michelle Diane Roberts
Randy Roebuck
Daniel Rolling
Lizzie Russell
Emily A. Sargent
Erin Catherine Schmitz
Colin M. Sebern
Nicholas Slatten
Clare Sobetski
Matt Stiles
Kelly R. Sumrall
Kaitlyn Tekip
Julia Ann Thompson
Naiomy Torres
Audrey M. Vertovec
Amanda Faith Vitry
Daniel J. Weisiger
Christina Wells
Jessica Wells

Rachel Ann Wells
Marcus K. Wells
Devon Christopher White
Kathryn A. Williams
Christopher Hayden Wright
Alexis Yates
Kelly Zimmerman

Teacher Participants

Ann Marie Brna
Marilyn Bush
Diane S. Carrol
Mary Ellen Cohen
Mary Beth Coonan
Judith H. Cozzens
John J. Cozzens
Mary Cathleen Danielson
Roberta A. DeNieu
Kari Drumm
Mary Ernst
Joy A. Fitzgerald
Cathleen D. Golden
Marylou Golding
Tonja Gorrell
Elizabeth A. Healy
Amy E. Hogan

Sarah J. Hogan
Nancy L. Johnson
Zennetta E. Jones
Mary C. Kircher
Linda M. Knowlden
Sarah L. K. Lorentz
Elaine A. Noel
Kimberly O'Connor
Michele Pascente
Adrean M. Pepper
Carol Preziosi
Rose Roy
Anita J. Ryan
Phyllis Ryan
Br. Gary A. Sawyer, ECSA
Susan J. Shaver
Cheryl M. Thrun
Elaine Tucker
Rory K. Turra

Maureen E. Wetmore

Catherine A. Whitney

High School Mentors

Chaylyn E. Alexander

Bretten Jarmon Bennett

Michael DeNieu

Daniel P. Hogan

Mechelle Kim Lech

Andrew C. McCartin

Sarah Marie Moran

Jessica E. Polak

Carrie E. Preziosi

Matthew Robinson

Mary Nichole Noah Stipe

Eileen Elizabeth Walford

Erika Justine Wells

Photographers

Ron Horn

Lillian LaFleur

Al Mida

Volunteers

James Baca

Msgr. Thomas P. Barry

Mary Baylie

Bill Beckman

Noreen Begordis

Fran Billars

Deacon Frank Bocovich

Craig Bowman

Betsy Boyle

Joe Brath

Pam Bruin

Rev. Joseph Cao

Archbishop Charles J. Chaput

Leanne Coffey

Rev. Andrew Cozzens

Julie Deanda

Theresa Donnelly

Jerry Drumm

Ed Duggan

Norma Ferrufino

Zee Ferrufino

Kathy Fisher

Rev. Robert Fisher

Cathy Fleming

Adrian Flores

Michelle Fromme

Marion Fuller

Rev. Fred Gaglia

Chester Gilliam

Edyie Glapion

Rev. Francis Gloudeman

Dr. Joseph Gloudeman

Bishop José Gomez

Patty Greenberg

Kathy Grywusiewicz

Sr. Dorothy Guadalupe

Gloria Guadreault

Loraine Guitterez

Shannon Gunning

Patty Hagen

Kimberly Hahn

Helen C. Healy

Bernadette Henderson

Judy Hogan

Rev. Walter Huber

Marty Hutt

Rev. Michael Joncas

Rev. Simon Kalonga

Rev. Andrew Kimberling

Thad Kingston

Cynthia Kuznia

Julie LaChance

Nora Lawler

Eileen Lech

Lisa Lavario

Barb Loetz

Eileen Love

Rev. Tom Margevicius

Annette Martinez

Lee Martinez

Carl Maschka

Alfred Matayo

Rosemary McCabe

Pat McCartin

Bev McConaughey

Theresa McCullar

Maureen McHugh

Kim Meyer

Sr. Ignatius Miceli

Ruby Moscoso

Susan Murphy

Shannon Naughton

Maureen O'Brien

Corrine O'Donnell

Dr. Vern Ostdiek

Jane Peloquin

Kelly Perez

Sr. Illaria Povero

Jennifer Radcliffe

Rev. Robert Reycraft

Rose Ann Schickling

Richard Schuh

Florence Sebern

Brother Simon

Lu Stiles

Sr. Joanna Strouse

Sr. Francis Teresa

Sr. Maria Bernard Tran

Sr. Anna Truong

Mary Ann Walford

Rev. Gabriel Weber

Terry Wells

Rev. Jeff Wilborn

Michael Woodward

Dale Zalmstra

Archbishop Vehr Library Staff

Denver Archdiocese Dept. of Education

St. Louis School Staff

If you'd like to learn more about other American cultures and topics such as African Americans, Hispanic Americans, Japanese Americans, Jewish Americans, special needs and young heroes, look into the other *Kids Explore Series* books. For more information, your parents may call (303) 795-0050.

Pauline
BOOKS & MEDIA

The Daughters of St. Paul operate book and media centers at the following addresses. Visit, call or write the one nearest you today, or find us on the World Wide Web, www.pauline.org

CALIFORNIA
3908 Sepulveda Blvd, Culver City, CA 90230   310-397-8676
5945 Balboa Avenue, San Diego, CA 92111   858-565-9181
46 Geary Street, San Francisco, CA 94108   415-781-5180

FLORIDA
145 S.W. 107th Avenue, Miami, FL 33174   305-559-6715

HAWAII
1143 Bishop Street, Honolulu, HI 96813   808-521-2731
Neighbor Islands call: 800-259-8463

ILLINOIS
172 North Michigan Avenue, Chicago, IL 60601   312-346-4228

LOUISIANA
4403 Veterans Memorial Blvd, Metairie, LA 70006   504-887-7631

MASSACHUSETTS
Rte. 1, 885 Providence Hwy, Dedham, MA 02026   781-326-5385

MISSOURI
9804 Watson Road, St. Louis, MO 63126   314-965-3512

NEW JERSEY
561 U.S. Route 1, Wick Plaza, Edison, NJ 08817   732-572-1200

NEW YORK
150 East 52nd Street, New York, NY 10022   212-754-1110
78 Fort Place, Staten Island, NY 10301   718-447-5071

OHIO
2105 Ontario Street, Cleveland, OH 44115   216-621-9427

PENNSYLVANIA
9171-A Roosevelt Blvd, Philadelphia, PA 19114   215-676-9494

SOUTH CAROLINA
243 King Street, Charleston, SC 29401   843-577-0175

TENNESSEE
4811 Poplar Avenue, Memphis, TN 38117   901-761-2987

TEXAS
114 Main Plaza, San Antonio, TX 78205   210-224-8101

VIRGINIA
1025 King Street, Alexandria, VA 22314   703-549-3806

CANADA
3022 Dufferin Street, Toronto, Ontario, Canada M6B 3T5   416-781-9131
1155 Yonge Street, Toronto, Ontario, Canada M4T 1W2   416-934-3440

¡También somos su fuente para libros, videos y música en español!